Using Statistics in Teaching Physical Education
A LINEAR PROGRAMMED PRESENTATION

Using Statistics in Teaching Physical Education
A LINEAR PROGRAMMED PRESENTATION

KENNETH A. PENMAN
Professor of Physical Education
Washington State University

JOHN WILEY AND SONS
New York   London   Sydney   Toronto

Copyright © 1976, by John Wiley & Sons, Inc.

All rights reserved. Published simultaneously in Canada.

No part of this book may be reproduced by any means, nor transmitted, nor translated into a machine language without the written permission of the publisher.

Library of Congress Cataloging in Publication Data:

Penman, Kenneth A
  Using statistics in teaching physical education.

  Includes indexes.
  1. Physical education and training—Statistical methods—Programmed instruction. I. Title.
GV342.5.S7P45   613.7′01′82   76-3703
ISBN 0-471-67916-X

Printed in the United States of America

10 9 8 7 6 5 4 3 2 1

Preface

This book is a programmed unit in beginning statistics, with special emphasis on how statistics can be used in teaching. The content is consistent with materials found in most tests and measurements books in physical education; however, it is presented in a linear programmed format so that you can master the material on a self-instructional basis. Programmed texts are making rapid headway as a teaching method because they provide an interesting and fun way to learn. The book is designed around one of the basic principles of learning—immediate feedback.

When a course or unit of instruction is programmed, it is broken down into very minute and carefully arranged steps through which you reason your way, one small step at a time. In addition to exercises at the end of each unit, you are constantly required to make mental and physical responses with each "bit" of information that is presented. Every step or frame calls for a written response, which requires both thinking and concentration. By thinking through each "bit" of information and making responses as you go, you soon find that you mastered a concept that originally appeared to be rather complicated.

It is not necessary to check with other students or with your teacher in order to find out if you are progressing properly. The program provides an immediate check to make sure that you have understood. The more often reinforcement takes place and the more quickly it follows the writing of your response, the better you learn.

Finally and probably most important, is that you can proceed as rapidly or as slowly as you wish. There is no need to wait on slower students; or, if this kind of material comes slower to you, you do not have to rush, feel you are slowing down the class or feel embarrassed by asking questions.

The material in this program has been field tested in tests and measurements classes for four years. Students with varied abilities have found it to be a stimulating way to learn (what to many is) a difficult subject.

Kenneth A. Penman

How to Use the Book

Each step is called a frame. All frames are numbered consecutively in each set for quick reference. Each frame requires you to do something. Generally you are to recall a word or pair of words, or make a simple calculation. Immediately after you have *written* the response or made the calculation, you lower the "mask" (this is a loosely inserted card) and check the correctness of your response. The top edge of the mask is placed at the top of each page, and lowered to the * * * line.

Whenever you are not sure about the correct answer to a frame, read the frame very carefully again. Many of the frames contain clues that guide you to the right answer. You probably will not make too many errors. When you do, reread the frame then, if you still do not understand the desired response, consult with your instructor. Take as much time as you wish in determining what your answer will be, but once you write your answer, immediately check the correctness of your response. The quicker you check your answer, the quicker you learn. Even the lapse of a few seconds can make a difference.

Each set represents approximately $1\frac{1}{4}$ hours' work. It is desirable to complete one set in a study session. Frequent interruptions will make learning the material less efficient.

All of the calculations in this book can be done by hand with little effort. However, if you have a calculator available, use it.

Your instructor will tell you how you are to use the program in the course. Some instructors prefer to use the program only, omitting the chapter or chapters in the regular course text. Some use the program in addition to the text, and some use part of the program and part of the text. The two sets in the Appendix are related to remedial arithmetic. If you have not used much arithmetic or elementary algebra for some time, it would be advisable for you to begin immediately with the exercises in the Appendices. Unfortunately, statistics books do not use the same symbols to represent means, standard deviation, etc. The symbols used in this text represent the latest attempt to unify statistical symbols.

Good Luck!

K. A. P.

Contents

set	1	ORGANIZATION OF DATA	2
set	2	VARIABLES AND THEIR MEASUREMENT	16
set	3	MEASURES OF CENTRAL TENDENCY FOR UNGROUPED DATA	30
set	4	VARIABILITY OF UNGROUPED DATA	44
set	5	CORRELATION—UNGROUPED DATA	62
set	6	THE NORMAL DISTRIBUTION CURVE	82
set	7	THE MEAN AND STANDARD DEVIATION WITH GROUPED DATA	106
set	8	CORRELATION WITH GROUPED DATA	128
set	9	CALCULATING PERCENTILES WITH GROUPED DATA	150
set	10	GRADING SYSTEMS	168
set	11	COMPARING GROUP PERFORMANCE	192
set	12	GRAPHIC PRESENTATION OF DATA	214

Appendixes

	A.	CALCULATION OF SQUARE ROOT	234
	B.	ELEMENTARY ALGEBRAIC PROCEDURES	248
	C.	FORMULAS	264
		INDEX	268

Using Statistics in Teaching Physical Education
A LINEAR PROGRAMMED PRESENTATION

SET 1
Organization of Data

The term statistics has often been referred to as "the numbers game." The reason for this is that the discipline of statistics is concerned with the analysis or examination of a group of numbers. The numbers may be scores received on a skill test, batting averages, scores from a knowledge test, and the like. When a teacher obtains a set of numbers they are called data. A single score would be called a raw score or datum.

In Set 1 we will be concerned with how we can organize scores in a logical order and how these data are classified in a hierarchical system.

OBJECTIVES

After completion of this set you must be able to:

1. Define the terms: data, raw score, ordinal numbers and cardinal numbers.
2. List the four levels of measurement.
3. Identify to which level of measurement specific kinds of data belong.

---

1. In physical education we are constantly obtaining measurements of various characteristics for groups of individuals. When you measure the age, height, weight, or skill level of a group of individuals you obtain a set of numbers. The technical term used to describe a set of

4 Using Statistics in Teaching Physical Education

numbers is data. If we were to measure skill in serving a badminton bird, the set of numbers we collected would be called _____.

* * *

data

---

2. The term *raw score* is used to indicate a measurement of some type for a single student. If a student received a score of 14 on a badminton serve test, this would be called his _____ _____.

* * *

raw score

---

3. The raw scores make up what we call the _____ for any specific measure.

* * *

data

---

4. Since students vary in their ability to serve in badminton, would you expect the raw scores of a group to vary or to be identical? _____ _____.

* * *

to vary

---

5. When you gather data on a large number of students you find the __ _____ for each individual may be different.

* * *

raw score

---

6. **Plate 1**

    Badminton serve test scores for ten students:

    10, 7, 14, 8, 6, 9, 9, 11, 13, 8

    These individual numbers are called _____ _____, whereas the group of numbers is called _____.

    * * *

    raw scores, data

7. The first step in describing a set of numbers is generally to arrange them in some kind of order. Rearrange the numbers in Plate 1 so that the numbers are listed from lowest to highest. _____ _____.

    * * *

    6, 7, 8, 8, 9, 9, 10, 11, 13, 14

8. Within the set of data found in Frame 7, which raw scores appear twice? _____.

    * * *

    8 and 9 each appear twice

9. Numbers vary also in kind. Some numbers describe a category, some numbers are relative to each other and some numbers have exact values. In the "numbers game" numbers are categorized according to their relative "sophistication" into what we call *level of measurement*. There are four levels: the nominal scale, the ordinal scale, the interval scale and the ratio scale.

    In the measurement hierarchy there are how many levels of measurement? _____.

    * * *

    four

6 Using Statistics in Teaching Physical Education

10. The first level, or most simple scale of measurement, is called the nominal scale (nom means name). This scale uses numbers to describe or name categories. For example, in football we use numbers in the 40's to designate fullbacks, 60's for guards, 70's for tackles, 80's for ends, and so on. A player whose number is 86, of course, is not twice as good, or valuable, as a player whose number is 43. Instead, numbers on the nominal scale only do what? _____

_____ .

* * *

describe or name categories

---

11. The lowest level of measurement, that which merely describes a category, is called the _____ _____ .

* * *

nominal scale

---

12. Another example of the nominal scale would be car license plate numbers. Certain numbers indicate a county in which the car is registered.

    Why would these numbers be examples of the nominal scale? _____

_____ .

* * *

because they name or describe a category

---

13. The next level of measurement is called the ordinal scale. It is called the ordinal scale because the numbers have a ranked value. First place is better than third place, although we may not know by how much.

Raw scores or numbers that are ranked in order of preference are measurements at the _____ level of measurement.

* * *

ordinal

---

14. The order of finish in a cross country meet would be an example of data being measured at the ordinal level because their place is determined not by their exact time, but by their _____.

* * *

rank

---

15. In quite a few contests in physical education, particularly in track and field and swimming, team points are awarded on the basis of the rank or relative position for which each performer finishes. These are measurements at the _____ level.

* * *

ordinal

---

16. Ordinal numbers are defined as any of the numbers (first, second, third, etc.) that imply rank. Cardinal numbers (one, two, three, etc.) imply exact value. Cardinal numbers may be used in arithmetic operations, but ordinal numbers may not. For example, the cardinal number 4 can be divided by the cardinal number two. However, the ordinal number fourth cannot logically be divided by the ordinal number second.

Which of the following are ordinal numbers and which are cardinal?

   a. six, seven   _____

   b. third, fourth   _____

8 Using Statistics in Teaching Physical Education

* * *

a. cardinal
b. ordinal

---

17. Ordinal numbers can be defined as _____

_____.

* * *

numbers that indicate relative position

---

18. Cardinal numbers can be defined as _____

_____.

* * *

numbers that have exact value

---

19. The first level of measurement is called the _____ scale. The second level of measurement is called the _____ scale.

* * *

nominal, ordinal

---

20. Define in your own words what nominal and ordinal levels of measurement mean. _____

_____

_____

_____

_____.

* * *

Your answer should be something like:

Nominal level: The nominal level of measurement uses numbers to describe categories.

Ordinal level: The ordinal level of measurement uses numbers to indicate rank.

---

21. In column A there are several nominal and ordinal measures. Indicate which kind of measures are of that level.

Column A	Level of Measurement
a. football league standings	
b. varsity team	
c. basketball player	
d. finish place in 40 yard dash	

* * *

a. football league standings	ordinal
b. varsity team	ordinal
c. basketball player	nominal
d. finish place in 40 yard dash	ordinal

---

22. The third level of measurement is called the interval scale. This scale is better than the ordinal scale because it tells you how much better a person is than another. The measurements used in this category have equal intervals. For example, if you measured the temperature of two track men at rest, had them run 4 miles, then remeasured their temperature and found that one boy's temperature increased by 4 degrees Fahrenheit and the other increased by 2 degrees Fahrenheit, you could say that one increase was twice as much as the other.

The scale that tells you which score ranks highest and by how much is called the _____ scale.

10 Using Statistics in Teaching Physical Education

* * *

interval

---

23. With the interval scale, the values within the scale of numbers are equal. An increase in temperature on the basketball court from 70 degrees to 75 degrees is an increase of 5 degrees. An increase from 80 to 85 degrees is also 5 degrees. With this scale, however, there is no true zero point.

    Another major characteristic of the interval scale is that there is no true zero.

    What are the three major characteristics of the interval scale? _____

    _____

    _____

    _____.

* * *

1. rank is implied
2. equal intervals
3. no true zero point

Note. In general, the statistical operations allowable with data at the interval level are similar to those allowable with ratio level measures, which will subsequently be discussed. There are technical differences that are beyond the scope of this text.

---

24. The highest level of measurement is called the ratio scale. Measurements in this category fall on a scale that has direction, equal intervals and a true zero point. Fortunately, in physical education most of our measurements fall into this category (height, weight, age, scores on skill tests, etc.). Because the scale has equal intervals and a true zero point, all arithmetic operations are permissible (addition, subtraction, multiplication and division) with the data. All arithmetic operations are permissible with data on the _____ scale.

Organization of Data 11

* * *

ratio

---

25. Occasionally, it is not clear whether data should be considered at one level or another. Heart rate, for example, depends on whether the assumption is made that the person is alive. Merely counting heart rate always begins with zero. That measurement is rate/minute but is measured on a scale that begins at zero (a ratio scale). Live humans, however, have a range of normal rate between 40–100 beats/minute (an interval scale because no living human would have a heart rate of zero).

Heart rate could be considered on the _____ or ____ _____ level of measurement.

* * *

interval or ordinal

---

26. When we measure the weight of eleventh grade boys we are using the ratio scale because the scale has _____ intervals and a true _____.

* * *

equal, zero

---

27. In column A there are several interval and ratio measures. Indicate which kind of measures are of that level.

Column A   Level of Measurement
a. reaction time
b. batting average
c. visual acuity
d. intelligence

a. reaction time	ratio
b. batting average	ratio
c. visual acuity	interval
d. intelligence	interval

28. We can calculate means, measures of variability, correlations, scale scores, for example, with most data in physical education because most of the measurements we take are on the _____ scale.

* * *

ratio

EXERCISES FOR SET 1

1. Define the following terms:
   a. raw score
   b. data
   c. ordinal numbers
   d. cardinal numbers
2. List the four levels of measurement in order from lowest to highest.
3. The four levels of measurement are listed in column B. In column A there are several types of measurements. Find the level of measurement that best relates to the type of measurement found in column A.

	Column A	Column B
a. _____ team standing	1. nominal
b. _____ height	2. ordinal
c. _____ sex	3. interval
d. _____ tennis serve test	4. ratio

Continued

Column A (Continued) Column B

e. _____ age 1. nominal

f. _____ football position 2. ordinal

g. _____ intelligence quotient 3. interval

h. _____ temperature 4. ratio

i. _____ weight

j. _____ basketball free throws

k. _____ placing in 100 yard freestyle

ANSWERS FOR SET 1 EXERCISES

1. a. an individual number, score or datum
   b. a set of numbers or raw scores
   c. numbers that indicate relative position (e.g., first, second)
   d. numbers that represent exact values (e.g., one, two, three)
2. nominal, ordinal, interval, ratio
3. a. 2
   b. 4
   c. 1
   d. 4
   e. 4
   f. 1
   g. 3
   h. 3
   i. 4
   j. 4
   k. 2

SET 2
Variables and Their Measurement

Up to this point we have been discussing what constitutes a set of data. In general we have been referring to one type of measurement, for example, weight or height. Any quantity of some thing that can be measured is called a variable. Height, weight, strength, intelligence, sex, eye and hair color, or time in the 100 yard dash, are all variables.

In this set we will learn the characteristics of discrete and continuous variables and some rules associated with reporting continuous variables.

OBJECTIVES

After completion of this set you must be able to:
1. Define a discrete variable.
2. Define a continuous variable.
3. Differentiate variables as to whether they are discrete or continuous.
4. Know how to state the accuracy of a variable.
5. Know how to state the sensitivity of a variable.

---

1. Variables are characteristics of persons or things. Hair color, reaction time, sex, and skill as measured by some performance test are examples of variables.

18 Using Statistics in Teaching Physical Education

The word used to describe the characteristic of a person or thing is called a _____.

* * *

variable

---

2. There are two types of variables, discrete and continuous. Discrete variables are defined as measures that can take on only separated values. Separated values mean that there cannot be any fraction or "in between" value. Examples of discrete variables are sex, skill in performance when measured by acquisition of points on trials, and the number of participants on a team. There are only five members on a basketball team (playing at one time) and there can never be $4\frac{1}{2}$ or $5\frac{1}{2}$ or $5\frac{1}{4}$ players.

Which of the following sets of data are discrete variables?
   a. 3.5, 6.7, 13.624
   b. 3, 6, 14

* * *

b.

---

3. Because no partial credit should be given for $\frac{1}{2}$ chin-up, the number of chin-ups a student can do would be a _____ variable.

* * *

discrete

---

4. The second type of variable is called a continuous variable. A continuous variable is defined as a measure that can take on any value within a certain range.

Continuous variables are quantities such as hair or eye color, height, weight, or reaction time, where the increments form a continuum. For example, if a person says he weighs between 150 and 151 pounds, he

Variables and Their Measurement   19

can actually weigh any fraction of the one pound differential. Increments of continuous variables form a _____.

What are the two types of variables? _____

_____.

* * *

continuum
discrete, continuous

---

5. Because reaction time can be measured to any fraction of a second, it is what kind of variable? _____.

* * *

continuous

---

6. Five variables are listed below. Indicate whether they are discrete or continuous by placing a D or C in front of each variable.

   a. _____ batting average
   b. _____ number of errors
   c. _____ reaction time
   d. _____ varsity letters earned
   e. _____ cooperation

* * *

a.	C
b.	D
c.	C
d.	D
e.	C

20 Using Statistics in Teaching Physical Education

7. Continuous variables are only limited by the accuracy desired and limits of the instrumentation. In physical education we are interested in a person's height "to the nearest inch." If we were conducting research involving the relationship of height to something, it might be important to measure more accurately.

Often we may desire a great degree of accuracy in measurement, however, we do not have the instrumentation to record the data to the desired accuracy.

Continuous variables are limited in part by what two factors? _____
_____ .

* * *

accuracy desired, instrumentation

8. Many calculators have dials with which one can select a desired accuracy up to nine decimal points. Some electronic timers discriminate within 1/10,000 of a second. Most often, however, in physical education, this accuracy is not necessary; and in addition, the equipment necessary for such accuracy is quite expensive. Most calculations in handling data in physical education can be rounded off to two decimal places and most stop watches used can be read to the nearest 1/100 second.

The limits of the measuring instruments and the precision one desires are the two limiting factors in the accuracy of _____ variables.

* * *

continuous

9. Why is it unlikely to know the exact value of a continuous variable?

Variables and Their Measurement   21

_____
_____.

* * *

Your answer should be something like:
The actual value of a continuous variable is never really known because measurements, regardless of how accurate they are, always fall short of their exact value.

10. Even though we never know the exact value of a continuous variable, we have to report some kind of a figure. This figure is called the reported value.

    We never know the exact value of a continuous variable, so we use a _____ value.

* * *

reported

11. In your own words, define continuous and discrete variables. _____
    _____
    _____
    _____

* * *

Your answer should be something like:
Continuous variables can take on any value within a given range, whereas discrete variables can take on only separated values.

12. The limit imposed on a reported value of a continuous variable is called the sensitivity of the measuring process.

22 Using Statistics in Teaching Physical Education

The sensitivity of a measuring process is represented by the smallest unit of the reported scale of the measuring instrument. The sensitivity of 1.326 inches would be to the nearest _____ of an inch.

* * *

thousandth

---

13. Reported values have limits, which are referred to as the _____ of the measuring process.

* * *

sensitivity

---

14. The sensitivity of a weight measure of 64.2 pounds is to the nearest _____ of a pound.

* * *

tenth

---

15. The smallest unit of a reported measurement is called the _____ of the measuring process.

* * *

sensitivity

---

16. Often we wish to establish limits around a reported value within which the exact value lies. If we measure the weight of a wrestler to be 130 pounds, what are the lowest and highest actual weights that will result in a reported value of 130 pounds if the sensitivity is to the nearest pound?

Variables and Their Measurement

Rule. The limits for the exact value around any reported value are found by adding to and subtracting from the reported value one half of the sensitivity of the measuring process from the reported value.

The wrestler's reported weight was 130 pounds and sensitivity was to the nearest pound. The exact value would appear within the limits 129.5–130.5. If the wrestler's reported weight was 192 pounds, and sensitivity was to the nearest pound, the exact value would appear within what limits? _____.

* * *

191.5–192.5

---

17. The limits were found by subtracting and adding what to the reported value? _____.

* * *

half the sensitivity

---

18. If we time a student in the 220 yard dash at 26.7 seconds the sensitivity is to the nearest _____.

* * *

tenth (of a second)

---

19. The exact time elapsed for the student to run the 220 yard dash was actually somewhere between _____ and _____.

* * *

26.65 and 26.75 seconds

20. If we measured age for athletic classification and a student was 16 years old, the limits of his exact age would be _____ and _____.

* * *

15.5 and 16.5 years

21. If the student's age was reported as being 16.1 years, what would be the limits within which his exact age would fall if the sensitivity desired was .2 years? _____.

* * *

16.0 and 16.2 years

22. If a continuous variable, reaction time, was reported as 5.6 seconds and the sensitivity was the nearest $\frac{2}{10}$ second, what would be the limits within which the exact value would occur? _____ and _____?

* * *

5.5 and 5.7 seconds

23. Because a measure of time can take on any value within a specified range, it is called a _____ variable.

* * *

continuous

24. Any measurement that counts cardinal numbers, and can take on only separated values, is called a _____ variable.

* * *

discrete

EXERCISES FOR SET 2

1. Define a discrete variable.

2. Define a continuous variable.

3. In the following list of variables, mark a "C" if the variable is continuous and a "D" if the variable is discrete.

   a. _____ number of free throws made out of ten

   b. _____ aggressiveness

   c. _____ height

   d. _____ heart rate

   e. _____ temperature

   f. _____ time in a 100 yard race

   g. _____ age

   h. _____ strength

26 Using Statistics in Teaching Physical Education

4. In the table below insert the missing information.

Variable	Sensitivity of measurement	Reported value	Limits of exact value
a. elapsed time	nearest 2/10 second	9.6 sec	
b. weight		150 lb	147–153 lb
c. reaction time	nearest 1/100 second		0.525–0.535 second
d.	nearest 1/2 yr	13 yr 3 mo	13 yr, 0 mo 13 yr, 6 mo
e. water temperature	nearest degree Fahrenheit	84°	

ANSWERS FOR SET 2 EXERCISES

1. Discrete variables are measures that can take on only separated values.
2. Continuous variables are measures that can take on any value within a given range.
3. a. D
   b. C
   c. C
   d. D
   e. C
   f. C
   g. C
   h. C

4. a. 9.5–9.7 seconds
   b. nearest 6 pounds
   c. .53 seconds
   d. age
   e. 83.5–84.5 degrees Fahrenheit

SET 3

Measures of Central Tendency for Ungrouped Data

In physical education, data may come from numerous sources, such as skill tests, knowledge tests and physical measurements. The first step in the analysis of these data is to determine the one score value that best describes the entire distribution of scores. In statistical terms this one score is called a measure of central tendency because it is the central value around which the scores cluster. There are three commonly used measures of central tendency: the mode, the median and the mean. The method of determining these measures of central tendency for ungrouped data will be presented in this set. The term "ungrouped data" refers to a group of scores usually less than 30 in number. This number is rather arbitrary, however, and varies primarily on the availability of a calculator. Examining data where large numbers of scores are present will be discussed in a later set.

OBJECTIVES

After completion of this set you must be able to:
1. Define the terms: mode, median and mean.
2. Locate the mode of a set of scores.
3. Locate the median of a set of scores.
4. Calculate the mean for a group of scores using Formula 1.
5. Identify the following symbols:
$$N, \text{Mdn.}, \Sigma, X, \bar{X}$$

1. If we were to measure the weight of all eighth graders, we would find that they tend to group around some central or representative score. This representative score is called a measure of central tendency.

   The mode is defined as the most frequently occurring score in the distribution.

   Plate 2
   Weights of eighth grade boys arranged in ascending order:

   92, 97, 101, 105, 110, 110, 116, 122, 135, 142, 157

   What is the mode for this distribution of weights? _____.

   * * *

   110

2. Explain why the weight of 110 pounds is the mode of the distribution.

   _____

   _____.

   * * *

   because it is the score that occurs most frequently

3. The mode is a central or representative score.

   In more general terms, the mode is one of three measures of _____ _____.

   * * *

   central tendency

4. Occasionally a distribution of scores will not have a mode. More often, however, a distribution will have more than one mode. If a distribution has two modes, it is called a bimodal distribution.

Plate 3

Weights of tenth grade boys arranged in ascending order:

98, 101, 114, 115, 122, 122, 128, 136, 136, 147, 172, 195

List the mode(s) for this distribution. _____.

* * *

122 and 136

---

5. The distribution of scores in Plate 3 has two modes. Thus, it is called a _____ distribution.

* * *

bimodal

---

6. The distribution in plate 3 is bimodal because two scores occur _____ _____.

* * *

twice

---

7. The mode is a measure of central tendency; however, it does not tell you anything about how the scores are scattered about the measure of central tendency.

The mode only tells you what? _____
_____.

34 Using Statistics in Teaching Physical Education

* * *

which raw score occurs most frequently

---

8. The second measure of central tendency is called the median. It is defined as the midpoint of the distribution. Therefore, _____ % of the scores would fall above this measure, and _____ % would fall below it.

* * *

50, 50

---

9. What is the median height for the following distribution of high school senior girls? _____.

Plate 4

60, 62, 63, 64, 65, 67, 69

* * *

64

---

10. The median of a distribution in which there is an even number of scores will be a theoretical midpoint. The median for a distribution of six scores will be between the _____ and _____ scores.

* * *

3rd and 4th

---

11. The median height for the following distribution of high school senior girls is: _____.

Plate 5

60, 62, 63, 64, 65, 67

* * *

63.5

---

12. The symbol Mdn. is used for the median. The score of 64 in Plate 4 is the _____ (symbol) of the distribution.

* * *

Mdn.

---

13. The median differs from the mode in that the median is the _____ of a distribution, whereas the mode is the _____ of a distribution.

* * *

midpoint, most frequent score

---

14. In Plate 6 the mode is _____ and the median is _____.

Plate 6

59, 60, 62, 63, 63, 64, 65, 67, 69

* * *

63, 63

---

15. The third and most commonly used measure of central tendency is the mean. The mean is defined as the arithmetic average of the raw scores. The arithmetic average ($\bar{X}$) is found by dividing the sum (Σ)

36 Using Statistics in Teaching Physical Education

of the raw scores (X) by the number (N) of the scores in the distribution.

The arithmetic average is called the _____ .

* * *

mean

---

16. To obtain the mean, you add or sum all the raw scores and divide by

_____ .

* * *

N, the number of scores involved

---

17. The symbol that represents a single raw score is X. The symbol used to indicate summation, or the act of adding numbers together, is the Greek letter sigma (Σ).

What do you think ΣX means? _____

_____ .

* * *

that the individual raw scores in the distribution have been added.

---

18. Five boys, each, shot ten basketball free throws. They made the following number of shots, respectively:

Plate 7

6, 5, 3, 2, 4

What is the total number of points made by all five boys? $\Sigma X =$ ____ .

* * *

Measures of Central Tendency for Ungrouped Data 37

$$\Sigma X = 6+5+3+2+4 = 20$$

---

19. The symbol for the mean of a group of scores is $\overline{X}$, which is called bar X. The symbol for the arithmetic average is _____.

$$* * *$$

$$\overline{X}$$

---

20. In Plate 7, Frame 18, the boys' scores for shooting free throws were: 6, 5, 3, 2, and 4. The $\Sigma X = 20$. The mean is found by the formula:

Formula 1

$$\overline{X} = \frac{\Sigma X}{N}$$

Insert the data (raw scores of boys' basketball free throws) into Formula 1, and calculate the mean for the set of scores.

$$\overline{X} = \frac{\Sigma X}{N} =$$

$$* * *$$

$$\overline{X} = \frac{20}{5} = 4$$

---

21. To review, write out the formula for the measure of central tendency we call the mean, or arithmetic average:

$$* * *$$

$$\overline{X} = \frac{\Sigma X}{N}$$

22. The following scores were obtained as a result of administering a badminton serve test: 16, 20, 15, 17, 24 and 18.

    Using Formula 1, calculate the mean.

    * * *

    $$\bar{X} = \frac{\Sigma X}{N} = \frac{110}{6} = 18.33$$

---

23. As a review, match the following measures of central tendency with connecting lines.

    most frequent appearing score   median
    arithmetic average   mean
    midpoint of a distribution   mode

    * * *

    most frequent appearing score — median
    arithmetic average — mean
    midpoint of a distribution — mode

---

24. The following raw scores were obtained by nine girls on a field hockey shooting test:

    Plate 8

    3, 5, 6, 7, 7, 7, 8, 9, 11

    What is the mode? _____

What is the median? _____
What is the mean? _____

* * *

7, 7, 7

---

25. The fact that the mean, median and mode are the same in Frame 24 tells us that the scores are distributed very evenly. If we were to plot these scores on a graph we would find a very symmetrical curve. The greater the number of scores obtained, the greater the likelihood is that the measures of central tendency will be similar.

    In general, the measures of central tendency are more likely to be the same or close to the same when N is _____. (large or small?)

    * * *

    large

EXERCISES FOR SET 3

1. Define the mode.
2. Define the median.
3. Define the mean.
4. What symbol denotes the mean?
5. What symbol denotes the number of scores in a distribution?
6. What Greek letter describes the act of adding a group of numbers?
7. What symbol represents a single score or datum?
8. Find the mode, median, sum of scores, and mean for each of the following columns of raw scores.

40 Using Statistics in Teaching Physical Education

	A	B	C
	8	18	10
	7	15	10
	5	9	10
	5	7	9
	3	3	9
	2	2	9
			8
			7
			7
			7
			7
			6
			4

mode
Mdn.
ΣX
$\bar{X}$

ANSWERS FOR SET 3 EXERCISES

1. The mode is the most frequent score appearing in a distribution.
2. The median is the midpoint of the distribution of scores.
3. The mean is the arithmetic average of a group of raw scores.
4. $\bar{X}$
5. N
6. Σ (sigma)
7. X
8.

	A	B	C
mode	5	none	7
Mdn.	5	8	8
ΣX	30	54	103
$\bar{X}$	5	9	7.92

SET 4
Variability of Ungrouped Data

We have learned so far that data can be classified and ordered in various ways and that measures of central tendency can tell us which score the data cluster around. In this set we shall examine the dispersion or spread of the scores about the measure of central tendency.

The most commonly used measures for determining the variability or dispersion of scores about the measure of central tendency are the average deviation (variance) and the standard deviation. The range of scores is also used as a crude approximation of the variability of a group of scores.

The calculation of square root will be required in this unit. If you do not know how to calculate square root, turn now to Appendix A.

OBJECTIVES

After completion of this set the student must be able to:

1. Define variability.
2. List three commonly used measures of variability.
3. Identify the following symbols:
   a. $\Sigma(\bar{X} - X)^2$ b. AD c. σ
4. From a given set of ungrouped data, calculate:
   a. the range
   b. the sum of the deviations squared
   c. the average deviation

46   Using Statistics in Teaching Physical Education

   d. the standard deviation—method 1 using Formula 4
   e. the standard deviation—method 2 using Formula 5

---

1. We learned in Set 2 that all scores in a distribution are not the same, rather they vary. Measures of variability may be defined then as a measure of how scores vary or are scattered about the measure of central tendency.

   There are basically two reasons why a set of data will vary. One reason is that human beings are different individuals, with varying degrees of all variables. Secondly, most measurements are acquired by humans who are incapable of making perfect measurements (i.e., recording exact values).

   If ten girls are trying out for the position of softball pitcher, will the variable of pitching ability be the same numerical value for all girls? _____. Why or why not?

   _____

   _____.

* * *

no.
because all girls do not have the same ability
and measurements are imperfect

---

2. In the following sets of scores the mean is identical (10). Notice, however, how the scores vary about the mean in each case.

   Plate 9

$\overline{A}$	$\overline{B}$	$\overline{C}$
10	20	30
10	15	10
10	10	5
10	5	4
10	0	1

   In which column do the scores vary by the greatest amount _____. The least amount? _____.

Variability of Ungrouped Data   47

* * *

C, A

---

3. In your own words, define variability. _____
   _____.

* * *

Your answer should be something like:
    Variability is a measure of how great scores
    are scattered about the mean.

---

4. The most crude measure of variability, yet a quick approximation of how much a set of scores vary, is the *range* of the scores. The range is determined by Formula 2.

   Formula 2
   Range (R) = highest value — lowest value
                 + the sensitivity of the
                   measuring process

   Here are scores received by eight high school golfers:

   Plate 10
              118, 114, 88, 92, 105, 101, 89, 130

   What are the highest and lowest scores? _____ _____.

* * *

130 and 88

---

5. What was the sensitivity of the measuring process for the data in Plate 10? _____.

* * *

nearest stroke or 1

---

48 Using Statistics in Teaching Physical Education

6. What was the range of scores for the data in Plate 10? _____.

* * *

43 strokes

---

7. The most crude measure of variability is called the _____.

* * *

range

---

8. Plate 11 provides a set of data for reaction time in seconds of 6 third grade children.

    Plate 11

    1.32, 1.30, 1.26, 1.11, 1.16, 1.35

    What is the range? _____.

* * *

.25 seconds

---

9. Which of the following sets of scores for girls swimming the 50 yard free style had the greater variability as measured by the range? _____.

    Plate 12

1st period	2nd period
35.2	38.6
30.6	36.1
32.7	34.8
40.1	33.7
38.7	35.3
39.2	35.0

* * *

1st period

10. Most measures of variability use the mean ($\overline{X}$) as a reference point. The distance each single score is away from the mean becomes a contribution to the variability of the set of data. The variability of a set of data can be determined by finding the distance each score is away from the mean.

    $\overline{X} - X$ indicates the distance a raw score is away from the mean. The term may be also written $X - \overline{X}$.

    For each of the scores below, calculate $\overline{X} - X$ or $X - \overline{X}$.

    Plate 13

X	$\overline{X} - X$ or $X - \overline{X}$
9	+3
8	
6	
4	
3	
$\Sigma X = 30$	
$\overline{X} =$	

    * * *

    $$\overline{X} - X = -3, -2, 0, +2, +3$$
    $$\text{or } X - \overline{X} = +3, +2, 0, -2, -3$$

    Note. It does not make any difference whether you use $\overline{X} - X$ or $X - \overline{X}$, however, you should be consistent.

11. If we recall, however, the mean is defined as the arithmetic average. If we measure the distance away from the mean of each score found

above the mean and likewise for those scores below the mean, the result would be zero.

Plate 14

	distance each raw
$\bar{X} - X$ or	score is away from
$X - \bar{X}$	the mean

X	$X - \bar{X}$
9	3
8	2
6	0
4	−2
3	−3
$\Sigma X = 30$	$\Sigma(\bar{X} - X) = 0$

To eliminate the problem of the sum of the deviations away from the mean equaling zero, we can "sum the squares" of the deviations. The sum of squares is found by finding the difference each score is away from the mean, squaring each of those deviations, then adding the squared scores.

Complete the $(\bar{X} - X)^2$ column in Plate 15 and find $\Sigma(\bar{X} - X)^2$

Plate 15

X	$(\bar{X} - X)$	$(\bar{X} - X)^2$
9	3	9
8	2	
6	0	
4	−2	
3	−3	
$\Sigma X = 30$	$\Sigma(\bar{X} - X) = 0$	$\Sigma(\bar{X} - X)^2 =$
$\bar{X} = 6$		
	$\Sigma(\bar{X} - X)^2 = ?$	

26

12. In your own words, explain the three steps necessary for using the sum of squares of the deviations method to determine the variability of a set of data. _____

_____.

* * *

Your answer should be something like:
> Find the distance each score is away from the mean, square that number, then add all squared numbers.

13. What is the range of scores for each class and which class has greater variability in its scores? _____.

Plate 16

Basketball free throw accuracy.

Class 1	Class 2
1	2
7	3
5	3
4	6
3	4
	5
	5

* * *

7, 5, class 1

14. Now let's find the sums of the deviations squared for the two classes.

Plate 17

Class 1

X	$(\bar{X}-X)$	$(\bar{X}-X)^2$
1	3	
7	−3	
5	−1	
4	0	
3	1	
$\Sigma X = 20$		$\Sigma(\bar{X}-X)^2 = $ ─

$N = 5$

$$\bar{X} = \frac{\Sigma X}{N} = \frac{20}{5} = 4$$

Class 2

X	$(\bar{X}-X)$	$(\bar{X}-X)^2$
2	2	
3	1	
3	1	
6	−2	
4	0	
5	−1	
5	−1	
$\Sigma X = 28$		$\Sigma(\bar{X}-X)^2 = $ ─

$N = 7$

$$\bar{X} = \frac{\Sigma X}{N} = \frac{28}{7} = 4$$

* * *

Class 1 = 20, Class 2 = 12

---

15. Since $\Sigma(\bar{X}-X)^2$ is a sum, it is a function of the number of scores involved.

    In general, if there are more scores in one group than another, the $\Sigma(\bar{X}-X)^2$ will be greater for which—the larger or the smaller group?

    _____.

* * *

the larger group

---

16. In order to overcome this problem we can calculate the average deviation. This formula is:

Formula 3

$$AD = \frac{\Sigma(\bar{X}-X)^2}{N}$$

Substituting numbers into Formula 3 for the two groups of scores in Plate 16 (carry out the answer two decimal points):

Class 1	Class 2
$AD =$ _____	$AD =$ _____

* * *

Class 1 $AD = 4$, Class 2 $AD = 1.71$

---

17. Referring to the data in Plate 16, Class 1 had a range of scores of 7 and an average deviation of 4, whereas Class 2 had a range of 5 and an average deviation of 1.71. Do the two measures of variability show similar results? _____.

* * *

yes

---

18. The average deviation (AD) or the average distance each score is away from the mean is a measure of variability. This term is also called the variance or mean square.

The algebraic statement $\dfrac{\Sigma(\bar{X}-X)^2}{N}$ is known by what *three* names?

1. _____.
2. _____.
3. _____.

54 Using Statistics in Teaching Physical Education

* * *

    1. average deviation
    2. variance
    3. mean square

---

19. The variance and mean square are terms that mean the same thing as the average deviation, which in turn is a measure of _____.

* * *

variability

---

20. The standard deviation (Greek lower case letter sigma—σ) is the most stable index of variability and is found by simply extracting the square root of the average deviation. The formula for the standard deviation using this method (method 1) is:

Formula 4

$$\sigma = \sqrt{\frac{\Sigma(\bar{X}-X)^2}{N}}$$

The symbol for the standard deviation is _____.

* * *

σ

---

21. Referring to data from Frame 16 we find the standard deviation for the two groups.

Plate 18

    Class 1   Class 2
    $\sigma = \sqrt{4}$ $\sigma = \sqrt{1.71}$

* * *

$\sigma = 2, \sigma = 1.3$

Variability of Ungrouped Data 55

22. In Frame 13, the variability for Class 2 was smaller even though the number of scores was larger.

   The variability of a set of data is related to the spread or dispersion of the scores about the _____.

   * * *

   mean or measure of central tendency

---

23. By knowing the mean and standard deviation of a set of data, we know the score around which the set of scores cluster; and we know how widely the scores _____.

   * * *

   vary

---

24. The steps used thus far have shown one way of arriving at the standard deviation with the identification along the way of other less often used measures of variability. Another method (Method 2), which is more direct and sometimes easier to compute, will now be presented.

   The second method of calculating the standard deviation from the original scores is by Formula 5. There are not any new symbols.

   Formula 5

   $$\sigma = \sqrt{\frac{\Sigma X^2}{N} - \bar{X}^2}$$

   In Formula 5 the ΣX^2 means _____.

   * * *

   the raw scores squared—then totaled

   Note. ΣX^2 and $(\Sigma X)^2$ are *not* the same.

56 Using Statistics in Teaching Physical Education

X	X^2
1	1
2	4
3	9
4	16
$\Sigma X = 10$	$\Sigma X^2 = 30$
$(\Sigma X)^2 = 100$	

25. In Formula 5 the term $\overline{X}^2$ means _____.

* * *

the mean squared

26. In order to find the data for Formula 5, all we need to do is square each raw score, total these squared scores, and square the mean. In addition, we need to know _____.

* * *

the number (N) of scores

27. Here again, let's use the basketball free throw scores found in Plate 16 (Frame 13) to calculate the standard deviation. Solve the equation.

Plate 19

X	X^2
1	1
7	49
5	25
4	16
3	9
$\Sigma X = 20$	$\Sigma X^2 = 100$

$$\overline{X} = \frac{\Sigma X}{N} = \frac{20}{5} = 4$$

$$\sigma = \sqrt{\frac{\Sigma X^2}{N} - \overline{X}^2} \qquad \sqrt{} = \sqrt{} =$$

Variability of Ungrouped Data 57

* * *

$\sigma = 2$

28. Below are six scores obtained from a skill test. Calculate the standard deviation using both Formula 4 and Formula 5.

    Plate 20

X	$\overline{X}-X$ $X-\overline{X}$	$(\overline{X}-X)^2$ $(X-\overline{X})^2$	X^2
5			
7			
2			
7			
6			
4			

    Formula 4

    $$\sigma = \sqrt{\frac{\Sigma(\overline{X}-X)^2}{N}}$$

    Formula 5

    $$\sigma = \sqrt{\frac{\Sigma X^2}{N} - \overline{X}^2}$$

    * * *

    Formula 4 $\sigma = 1.91$ Formula 5 $\sigma = 1.91$

29. Formulas 4 and 5 are used to calculate the standard deviation of _____ (grouped or ungrouped) data?

    * * *

    ungrouped

58 Using Statistics in Teaching Physical Education

30. The best formula to use for calculating the standard deviation depends on the size of the numbers you are dealing with, the number of scores you are dealing with, and the availability of a calculator.

Which formula (4 or 5) would be best to use to calculate the standard deviation if you had 25 scores, two digit numbers, and no calculator available? _____ .

* * *

Formula 4 or Method 1

---

31. Match the following statements with their equivalent symbols by interconnecting lines.

The difference each score is away from the mean—squared—then totaled	$\overline{X}$
Range	R
Average deviation (variance)	AD
Standard deviation	σ
	$\Sigma(\overline{X}-X)^2$

* * *

The difference each score is away from the mean—squared—then totaled	$\overline{X}$
Range	R
Average deviation (variance)	AD
Standard deviation	σ
	$\Sigma(\overline{X}-X)^2$

EXERCISES FOR SET 4

1. Define the term variability.
2. List three commonly used measures of variability.
3. Identify the following symbols:
    a. $\Sigma(\overline{X}-X)^2$ b. AD c. σ

Variability of Ungrouped Data   59

4. Below you will find the number of strikes made by eight students for a three game series bowling. Find:
   a. _____ the mean
   b. _____ the range of scores
   c. _____ the sum of the deviations squared
   d. _____ the average deviation
   e. _____ the standard deviation using Formula 4
   f. _____ the standard deviation using Formula 5

X	$(\bar{X} - X)$	$(\bar{X} - X)^2$	X^2
7			
1			
11			
6			
12			
4			
2			
5			
$\Sigma X =$ ___	$\Sigma(\bar{X} - X) =$ ___	$\Sigma(\bar{X} - X)^2 =$ ___	$\Sigma X^2 =$ ___

Formula 4

$$\sigma = \sqrt{\frac{\Sigma(\bar{X} - X)^2}{N}}$$

Formula 5

$$\sigma = \sqrt{\frac{\Sigma X^2}{N} - \bar{X}^2}$$

60 Using Statistics in Teaching Physical Education

ANSWERS FOR SET 4 EXERCISES

1. Variability is a measure of how scores are dispersed or scattered.
2. Range, Average Deviation and Standard Deviation.
3. a. the difference each score is away from the mean—squared—then totaled.
   b. average deviation
   c. standard deviation
4. a. __6__   mean
   b. __12__   the range
   c. __108__   the sum of the deviations squared
   d. __13.5__   the average deviation
   e. __3.67__   the standard deviation using Formula 4
   f. __3.67__   the standard deviation using Formula 5

Check:

X	$(\bar{X}-X)$	$(\bar{X}-X)^2$	X^2
7	+1	1	49
1	−5	25	1
11	+5	25	121
6	0	0	36
12	+6	36	144
4	−2	4	16
2	−4	16	4
5	−1	1	25
$\Sigma X = \overline{48}$	$\Sigma(\bar{X}-X) = \overline{0}$	$\Sigma(\bar{X}-X)^2 = \overline{108}$	$\Sigma X^2 = \overline{396}$

$$\bar{X} = \frac{\Sigma X}{N} = \frac{48}{8} = 6$$

Formula 4

$$\sigma = \sqrt{\frac{\Sigma(\bar{X}-X)^2}{N}} = \sqrt{\frac{108}{8}} = 3.67$$

Formula 5

$$\sigma = \sqrt{\frac{\Sigma X^2}{N} - \bar{X}^2} = \sqrt{\frac{396}{8} - 6^2} = 3.67$$

SET 5
Correlation — Ungrouped Data

Thus far we have used statistics to determine measures of central tendency and variability. In other words, we are now able to see, to some extent, how any individual score "stands" in relation to the group of scores.

Often, in physical education, we also want to measure association or relationships between variables. The correlation coefficient is the technique most often used for this purpose, and in this set we will learn to compute correlations with ungrouped data using the rank order method and the Pearson product method. Correlations are used frequently to determine the validity, reliability and objectivity of knowledge and sports skills tests.

OBJECTIVES

At the conclusion of this set you should be able to:

1. Define:
   a. a correlation coefficient
   b. a coefficient of determination
2. Identify the following symbols:

   a. ρ d. Y
   b. r e. ΣXY
   c. X f. r^2

64   Using Statistics in Teaching Physical Education

3. Compute a coefficient of correlation for ungrouped data using the rank order method (Formula 6) with and without tied ranks.
4. Compute a coefficient of correlation for ungrouped data using the Pearson product method (Formula 7).

---

1. A correlation coefficient may be defined as a measure of the degree of agreement between two variables. In the previous sets we were primarily concerned with one set of data, that is one class of students had scores on one variable (X). When we compute a correlation we are measuring the degree of relationship for one class of students on two variables (X, Y).

    A simple correlation coefficient measures the degree of agreement between how many variables? _____.

    * * *

    two

---

2. In your own words, define a "correlation coefficient."

    _____

    _____

    _____.

    * * *

    Your answer should be something like:
    A measure of the degree of relationship
    between two variables.

---

3. A variable is generally designated by a capital letter. For example, the symbol X represents one variable and any other capital letter could represent another or second variable, for example, Y, Z, K, L. Usually the two variables under investigation in a correlation problem are designated arbitrarily as X and Y.

    You must identify which letter represents which variable. If we wish to investigate the relationship between height and weight and we designate the letter X for height, we would represent the variable weight with the letter _____.

* * *

Y
(or any other capital letter)

---

4. To determine the degree of relationship between two variables, we would calculate a _____ _____.

* * *

correlation coefficient

---

5. When the data we are using is at least at the ordinal level of measurement, we can use the rank order method to calculate quickly correlation coefficients.

To use the rank order method of correlation, we must have measurements at least at the _____ scale.

* * *

ordinal

---

6. Correlation coefficients fall within a range of +1.0 to −1.0. A plus 1.0 correlation would mean that there is perfect agreement between the two variables (e.g., the higher the body weight of a student, the greater his strength would be). What do you think a minus 1.0 correlation would indicate? _____
_____.

* * *

perfect *dis*agreement between two variables
(e.g., the higher the body weight of a student,
the *lower* his strength would be
—an inverse relationship)

---

7. Suppose we think there is a high relationship between body weight and strength. Assume that we weigh five high school seniors and

66 Using Statistics in Teaching Physical Education

measure their grip strength (or leg strength, etc.). Let X equal the variable weight and Y the variable strength.

Plate 21

student	X	Y
1	205	32
2	190	30
3	182	27
4	161	20
5	149	16

By studying the scores you will see that the heaviest was strongest, on down to the lightest being the weakest. What would this show between the two variables: perfect agreement (+1.0); perfect disagreement (−1.0); or no relationship (0)? _____

_____.

* * *

perfect agreement (+1.0)

8. Let's rearrange the scores in Plate 21 as follows:

Plate 22

student	X	Y
1	205	16
2	190	20
3	182	27
4	161	30
5	149	32

Since the scores are now inversely related, what can we say about the relationship between variables X and Y? _____

_____.

Correlation—Ungrouped Data 67

* * *

there is perfect disagreement (-1.0)

---

9. Generally, perfect agreement or disagreement is not found. The degree of association generally falls somewhere between the two extremes. If there was no pattern between the variables, (a random order of variables), there would be no relationship and a zero (0) correlation would occur.

   A correlation found to be zero (0) would indicate that _____ exists between the two variables.

   * * *

   no relationship

---

10. The degree of association between two sets of scores is difficult to see by eye when many scores exist and when there is a less than perfect relationship. The following formula is used to calculate the coefficient when the data are ranked.

    Formula 6

    $$\rho = 1 - \frac{6 \Sigma D^2}{N(N^2-1)}$$

    ρ is the symbol used to designate that a correlation has been computed by the rank order method. It is the Greek letter rho.

    What Greek letter (symbol) is used to designate a rank order correlation coefficient? _____.

    * * *

    ρ (rho)

---

11. The scores for weight and strength used in Frame 8 are listed below with each score ranked with the best (or most desirable score) being given a ranking of 1. Then the differences in ranks are shown in the D column.

68 Using Statistics in Teaching Physical Education

Plate 23

student	X (weight)	Rank for X	Y (strength)	Rank for Y	D Difference in ranks
1	205	1	16	5	4
2	190	2	20	4	2
3	182	3	27	3	0
4	161	4	30	2	2
5	149	5	32	1	4

Student number 4 had a ranking of _____ on the X variable (weight) and a ranking of _____ on the Y variable (strength).

* * *

4, 2

---

12. In Formula 6, the D represents the *difference in rank* between the two variables for each person. Then ΣD^2 would represent the sum of the differences in rank, squared.

The difference in rank is represented by the symbol _____.

* * *

D

---

13. Assume two teachers rated 5 gymnasts on a tumbling routine. Let variable X equal one teacher's rating, and Y the second teacher's rating.

Plate 24

student	X	Y	D	D^2
AK	3	2	1	1
BL	1	1	0	0
CM	2	4	2	4
DN	4	3	1	1
EO	5	5	0	0

$\Sigma D^2 = 6$

Correlation—Ungrouped Data 69

Using Formula 6, we can calculate a correlation coefficient to determine the amount of agreement between the two judges or teachers.

Formula 6

$$\rho = 1 - \frac{6\Sigma D^2}{N(N^2-1)} = 1 - \frac{6(6)}{5(5^2-1)} = 1 - \frac{36}{120} = +.70$$

The value ρ here measures the agreement or relationships between the two people in their judgment as to how the students performed.

What kind of relationship is indicated by the correlation coefficient $\rho = +.70$: fairly strong agreement, fairly strong disagreement, or a weak relationship? _____.

* * *

fairly strong relationship

---

14. If the correlation coefficient found in Frame 13 had been around .10, it would have meant what? _____

_____.

* * *

that there was weak agreement between
the two judges on which performers were best.

---

15. Look again at Formula 6, $\rho = 1 - \frac{6\Sigma D^2}{N(N^2-1)}$. When we determine a rank order correlation coefficient using Formula 6, do we use the raw scores or the ranks of the scores? _____

_____.

* * *

only the ranks of the scores
(When using Formula 6 it is important to remember
that only the rank order of scores is being analyzed. The
actual scores are *not* being used in the calculations.)

16. Now let's compare a set of reported values. We want to find out if the times the 5 boys received in the 100 yard dash correlate highly with the same boys' times in the 220 yard dash.

The first step in calculating a rank order correlation coefficient is to rank the reported values.

Rank the five boys on both variables. (Remember the fastest time or lowest value is better.)

Plate 25

Name	100 yard Dash Time	Rank	220 yard Dash Time	Rank
Paul	10.4		23.6	
Mack	10.0		22.1	
Tim	10.7		23.4	
Kevin	10.9		24.5	
Bill	10.3		22.7	

* * *

Name	100 yard Dash Rank	220 Dash Rank
Paul	3	4
Mack	1	1
Tim	4	3
Kevin	5	5
Bill	2	2

17. Now find D and D^2 for each student and ΣD^2.

Plate 26

Name	100 yard Dash Time	Rank	220 yard Dash Time	Rank	D	D^2
Paul	10.4		23.6			
Mack	10.0		22.1			
Tim	10.7		23.4			
Kevin	10.9		24.5			
Bill	10.3		22.7			

Correlation—Ungrouped Data   71

* * *

Name	100 yard Dash Time	Rank	220 yard Dash Time	Rank	D	D^2
Paul	10.4	3	23.6	4	1	1
Mack	10.0	1	22.1	1	0	0
Tim	10.7	4	23.4	3	1	1
Kevin	10.9	5	24.5	5	0	0
Bill	10.3	2	22.7	2	0	0
						$\Sigma D^2 = 2$

---

18. Using Formula 6, find the rank order correlation for the data in Frame 17.

$$\rho = 1 - \frac{6\Sigma D^2}{N(N^2 - 1)} = \underline{\qquad} =$$

* * *

$$\rho = 1 - \frac{6(2)}{5(5^2 - 1)} = +.90$$

---

19. One additional problem exists with ranking scores. It is very likely that two performance variables could be identical.

   Rule. Whenever scores are tied, those tied scores are given the mean value of the number of tied ranks.

   Plate 27

Example 1 Raw Score	Rank	Example 2 Raw Score	Rank
32	1	365	1
30	2	360	3
28	3.5	360	3
28	3.5	360	3
27	5	355	5
		350	6

72 Using Statistics in Teaching Physical Education

Rank the following times for the 100 yard dash:

Plate 28

10.4 (   ), 10.0 (   ), 10.9 (   ), 10.3 (   ), 10.4 (   )

* * *

10.4 (3.5), 10.0 (1), 10.9 (5), 10.3 (2), 10.4 (3.5)
(There were five scores so there had to be five places.
Since two tied, they took the mean value of the tied ranks.)

---

20. Another convenient method of assigning ranks is to list the number of ranks possible (number of scores), then cross off each place as a rank is assigned.

    The ranking has been started for the data below. Complete the ranking. The data represent errors made on a task, so the lowest number is most desirable.

    Plate 29
    Raw Score: 10, 12, 13, 13, 16, 19, 21, 21, 21, 26
    Rank: 1   2
    Ranks Available: 1̸, 2̸, 3, 4, 5, 6, 7, 8, 9, 10

* * *

Raw Score: 10, 12, 13, 13, 16, 19, 21, 21, 21, 26
Rank: 1   2 3.5 3.5   5   6   8   8   8 10

---

21. Now, suppose we change one score in Plate 25, Frame 16. Change Paul's score from 10.4 to 10.3.

Name	100 yard Dash Time	Rank	220 yard Dash Time	Rank	D	D^2
Paul	10.3		23.6	4		
Mack	10.0	1	22.1	1		
Tim	10.7		23.4	3		
Kevin	10.9		24.5	5		
Bill	10.3		22.7	2		

$$\Sigma D^2 = \overline{3.5}$$

Correlation—Ungrouped Data 73

Complete the missing ranks, find the differences in ranks, square each of those differences in rank, add the squared differences, and find ρ using Formula 6.

$$\rho = 1 - \frac{6\Sigma D^2}{N(N^2-1)} \qquad \rho = 1 - \underline{} =$$

* * *

$$\rho = .83$$
(Notice that the correlation dropped from .90 to .83 by changing one score.)

---

22. The second method of correlation computation we shall learn utilizes the raw scores directly. The formula looks complicated at first; however, there is only one new operation.

    Formula 7

    $$r = \frac{N\Sigma XY - (\Sigma X)(\Sigma Y)}{\sqrt{[N\Sigma X^2 - (\Sigma X)^2][N\Sigma Y^2 - (\Sigma Y)^2]}}$$

    Which factor in Formula 7 have we not used as yet? _____.

    * * *

    $$\Sigma XY$$

---

23. ΣXY has not as yet been used, but it is simply the sum of all the products of the two variables X and Y. The symbol for the sum of the products is _____.

    * * *

    $$\Sigma XY$$

---

24. In order to find the correlation coefficient using this formula, we need:

    $$N \quad \Sigma X \quad \Sigma X^2 \quad \Sigma Y \quad \Sigma Y^2 \quad \Sigma XY$$

    The symbol that represents the sum of the squares of the second variable is _____.

74 Using Statistics in Teaching Physical Education

* * *

$$\Sigma Y^2$$

---

25. The following scores represent data acquired by high school girls. The X variable represents the number of chin-ups each girl completed and the Y variable represents the number of push-ups completed. We want to know what kind of a relationship exists between the two variables.

Plate 30
Complete any missing calculations and substitute numbers for the symbols in Formula 7. (Don't try to complete the calculation yet.)

Name	X	X^2	Y	Y^2	XY
Sally	5	25	6	36	30
Jean	4	16	5	25	
Pat	8	64	7		
Alice	7		8		
Ann	6		6		36
Sue	9		8		72

$\Sigma X =$ $\Sigma X^2 = 271$ $\Sigma Y = 40$ $\Sigma Y^2 =$ $\Sigma XY = 270$

$$r = \frac{N\Sigma XY - (\Sigma X)(\Sigma Y)}{\sqrt{[N\Sigma X^2 - (\Sigma X)^2][N\Sigma Y^2 - (\Sigma Y)^2]}}$$

$$= \frac{}{\sqrt{[][]}}$$

* * *

$$r = \frac{6(270) - 39(40)}{\sqrt{[6(271) - 39^2][6(274) - 40^2]}}$$

26. Now solve for *r*.

* * *

.88

---

27. As you can see by now, this method can be rather tedious without a calculator. With only six people and using very small quantities, the numbers in the calculations became quite large. The method that you select for calculating a correlation coefficient depends on the accuracy desired, the size of the numbers, the availability of a calculator and the number of pairs of scores.

    In your own words, define a correlation coefficient.

    _____

    _____

    _____.

* * *

Your answer should be something like:
   A correlation coefficient is a measurement of the degree of relationship between two variables or sets of scores.

---

28. Correlation coefficients are used to determine relationships for many purposes in addition to examples shown in this unit. Correlation coefficients are also used to determine validity, reliability and objectivity of written and skill tests. Validity coefficients are obtained by correlating scores on a test with some criterion measure (e.g., experts' ratings or another test).
    Reliability coefficients are obtained by correlating sets of scores by the same students, given on two different occasions by the same instructor.
    Objectivity coefficients are obtained by correlating sets of scores by the same students, given on two different occasions by a different instructor.

Validity coefficients give an indication as to how well a test measures what it claims to measure, whereas reliability and objectivity coefficients give information regarding the consistency of performance by the students.

Many other computational methods of determining correlation coefficients are available; however, the rank order and the Pearson product moment methods are used most frequently with ungrouped data.

To determine relationships between any variables, including test validity, reliability and objectivity, one would calculate a _____ _____.

* * *

correlation coefficient

---

29. The "goodness" of a correlation coefficient (i.e., excellent, very high, moderate or low) is arbitrary. It depends on the kinds of variables being measured, measurement accuracy and the critical nature of the use of the statistic, to name but a few considerations.

    One important aid often used to interpret a correlation coefficient is the *Coefficient of Determination*. The Coefficient of Determination is a theoretical approximation of the amount of similar quantities found in the two variables under study. It is calculated by squaring the correlation coefficient (ρ^2 or r^2).

    In Frame 18 we found the correlation coefficient between running the 100 yard dash and running the 220 yard dash was .90. What would be the coefficient of determination? _____.

* * *

.81 ($.90^2$)

---

30. This coefficient of determination (.81) would be interpreted as follows: 81% of whatever makes a person fast in the 100 yard dash is also responsible for making him fast in the 220 yard dash. This "whatever" may be a composite of factors such as strength, explosive power, reaction time or desire to win.

Correlation—Ungrouped Data 77

In Frame 26, the correlation between the girls' ability to do pull-ups and push-ups was .88. What would be the coefficient of determination? _____.

* * *

.77 (.88²)

---

31. How would the coefficient of determination of .77 be verbalized? ___

_____

_____.

* * *

Your answer would be something like:
77% of whatever makes a girl able to do pulls-ups
also contributes to her ability to do push-ups
(probably, in this case, the "whatever" is
shoulder girdle and arm strength).

---

32. Define, in your own words, a coefficient of determination. _____

_____

_____

_____.

* * *

Your answer should be like:
A coefficient of determination is a statistic used to approximate the amount of similar quantities found in the two variables being studied.

If a correlation of .20 between running speed and visual acuity was found, the coefficient of determination would be .04. Therefore, since the two variables had only 4% in common, we can conclude that running speed is not related to visual acuity.

EXERCISES FOR SET 5

1. a. Define a correlation coefficient.
   b. Define a coefficient of determination.
2. Identify the following symbols by drawing a line from one symbol to it's definition.

Symbol	Definition
ρ	Second variable
r	Coefficient of determination
X	Rank order coefficient of correlation
Y	Coefficient of correlation
ΣXY	Sum of cross products
r^2	First variable

3. a. Calculate a rank order correlation coefficient using Formula 6 for the following data:

Subject	Shot Put (Rank)	Discus (Rank)	D	D^2
1	42	115		
2	44	120		
3	36	94		
4	28	100		
5	39	90		
6	45	102		

   Formula 6

   $$\rho = 1 - \frac{6 \Sigma D^2}{N(N^2 - 1)}$$

   b. Calculate the coefficient of determination for the correlation calculated in a.

4. a. Find a correlation coefficient for the following pairs of scores using Formula 7. Variable X represents trial 5 on a motor performance test and Y represents trial 10 of the same test.

Student	X	X^2	Y	Y^2	XY
1	2		5		
2	1		2		
3	4		7		
4	4		6		
5	3		3		
6	6		8		
7	5		4		

$\Sigma X = \overline{}$ $\Sigma X^2 = \overline{}$ $\Sigma Y = \overline{}$ $\Sigma Y^2 = \overline{}$ $\Sigma XY = \overline{}$

$$r = \frac{N\Sigma XY - (\Sigma X)(\Sigma Y)}{\sqrt{[N\Sigma X^2 - (\Sigma X)^2][N\Sigma Y^2 - (\Sigma Y)^2]}}$$

b. Calculate the coefficient of determination.

80 Using Statistics in Teaching Physical Education

ANSWERS FOR SET 5 EXERCISES

1. a. A correlation coefficient is a measure of the degree of agreement between two variables.
   b. A coefficient of determination is used as a measure of the amount of similar quantities found in the two variables under study.

2.

Symbol	Definition
ρ	Second variable
r	Coefficient of determination
X	Rank order coefficient of correlation
Y	Coefficient of correlation
ΣXY	Sum of products
r^2	First variable

(matched: ρ → Rank order coefficient of correlation; r → Coefficient of correlation; X → First variable; Y → Second variable; ΣXY → Sum of products; r^2 → Coefficient of determination)

3. a.

Subject	Shot Put	(Rank)	Discus	(Rank)	D	D^2
1	42	3	115	2	1	1
2	44	2	120	1	1	1
3	36	5	94	5	0	0
4	28	6	100	4	2	4
5	39	4	90	6	2	4
6	45	1	102	3	2	4
						$\Sigma D^2 = 14$

$$\rho = 1 - \frac{6 \Sigma D^2}{N(N^2-1)} = 1 - \frac{6(14)}{6(36-1)} = .60$$

b. $\rho^2 = .36$

4. a.

Student	X	X^2	Y	Y^2	XY
1	2	4	5	25	10
2	1	1	2	4	2
3	4	16	7	49	28
4	4	16	6	36	24
5	3	9	3	9	9
6	6	36	8	64	48
7	5	25	4	16	20
	$\Sigma X = 25$	$\Sigma X^2 = 107$	$\Sigma Y = 35$	$\Sigma Y^2 = 203$	$\Sigma XY = 141$

$$r = \frac{N\Sigma XY - (\Sigma X)(\Sigma Y)}{\sqrt{[N\Sigma X^2 - (\Sigma X)^2][N\Sigma Y^2 - (\Sigma Y)^2]}}$$

$$r = \frac{7(141) - 25(35)}{\sqrt{[7(107) - 25^2][7(203) - 35^2]}}$$

$$r = \frac{112}{\sqrt{124(196)}} = \frac{112}{155.9} = .72$$

b. $r^2 = .52$

SET 6
The Normal Distribution Curve

Whenever a large number of students are measured on a specific variable, we find that some students will perform at a very high level, some will perform at a low level, and the majority will fall somewhere between these extremes. If we were to plot the scores in a frequency distribution, the smoothed curve would be shaped like the silhouette of a bell. This bell-shaped curve is called the normal distribution curve and is useful to the physical educator because most of the variables we measure are normally distributed in this manner.

OBJECTIVES

At the conclusion of this set you should be able to:

1. State the relationship of the mean, median and mode in a normal distribution.
2. Calculate z scores.
3. Determine the percentage of scores and numbers of people lying between various deviation values using Table 1 (found on page 88).
4. Calculate sigma scale, Hull scale and T scale scores from a set of raw scores.

---

1. A frequency distribution (to be described in detail in Unit 12) that has a bell shape, is called a normal distribution curve because

84 Using Statistics in Teaching Physical Education

measurements of many variables that occur in nature are normally distributed in this manner. When this situation exists, the mean, median and mode will be the same. A standard bell shaped curve is also called a _____

_____ .

* * *

normal distribution curve

---

2. Suppose we measured the heights of 400 seventh grade girls.

   If their heights were distributed normally, the frequency distribution of their heights would be shaped like what? _____ .

   * * *

   a bell

---

3. Because so many variables are distributed in the form of the normal curve, mathematicians have derived certain functions of the curve that are helpful to the practitioner. In a normal curve the mean, median and mode coincide; therefore, _____% of the scores lie to the right of the mean, and _____% lie to the left of the mean.

   * * *

   50, 50

---

4. Plate 31

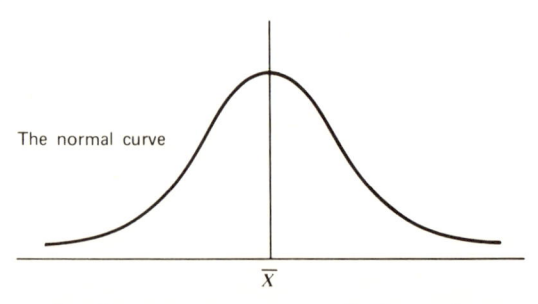

   The normal curve

   $\bar{X}$

   The area under the curve represents all the students or scores being measured on any particular variable. The total area under the normal curve, therefore, represents what percent of the people or scores? _____ %.

* * *

100%

5. Since the normal curve is symmetrical, and the mean and median are the same, how do the two halves of the curve compare? _____ _____.

* * *

they are identical
(or one half is a mirror image of the other)

6. In Set 4 we learned that the standard deviation was the most often used measure of variability. To review, what does variability measure? _____ _____.

* * *

the extent to which the scores deviate or vary from the mean

7. The standard deviation (σ) is always measured from the mean of the distribution of scores because it is a measure of the extent to which scores vary above and below the mean.

The field of mathematics has enabled us to know what percentage of the total group of scores fall in any designated area under the normal curve.

What percent of the scores on any variable would fall to the right of the $\overline{X}$ under the normal curve? _____.

* * *

50%

86 Using Statistics in Teaching Physical Education

8. Plate 32

[Normal curve with X and +1σ marked]

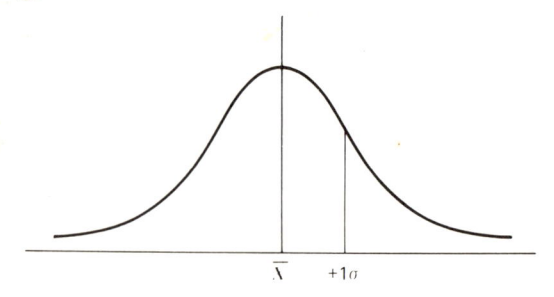

Plate 32 shows the area under the normal curve that represents one standard deviation above the mean. Scores above the mean are usually shown where, in relation to the mean? (The diagram above is typical.) _____

_____.

* * *

Scores above the mean are shown to the
right of the mean, on the baseline

9. Plate 33

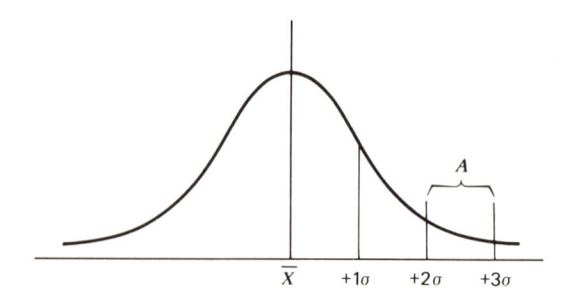

[Normal curve with X, +1σ, +2σ, +3σ marked, with area A between +2σ and +3σ]

Mathematicians have calculated the percentage of scores that fall under any given portion of the normal curve. For example, we know the percentage of scores that will be formed between 1 and 2 standard deviations away from the mean.

How would you describe the area of the normal curve labeled A? ___

_____.

The Normal Distribution Curve   87

* * *

the area lies between 2 and 3 standard
deviations above the mean

---

10. Any portion of the normal curve may be described by its distance, given in standard deviation units, from the mean.

The percentage of scores under any portion of the normal curve is given in Table 1. All values are percentage parts of the total area under the normal curve corresponding to distances on the base line between the mean and successive points from the mean in units of standard deviation.

Since all values in Table 1 are given in distances from the mean, would you expect the values to be different or the same for both halves of the normal curve? _____.

* * *

the same

---

11. In Table 1, the standard deviation units in tenths are listed in the left hand margin. Across the top of the table are columns labeled to the hundredth decimal place. If we wanted to know for example, what percent of the cases in a set of data will be found between the mean and .23 standard deviation unit, we would locate .2 in the left hand margin, .03 across the top of the table, then read the percentage of cases (09.10) or 9.1%.

Plate 34

Units	.00	.01	.02	.03	.04	.05
0.0						
0.1						
0.2				09.10		
0.3						

What percent of the cases in a set of data will be found between the mean and 1.3 standard deviation units? _____.

TABLE 1. Percentage Parts of the Total Area Under the Normal Probability Curve

Units	.00	.01	.02	.03	.04	.05	.06	.07	.08	.09
0.0	00.00	00.40	00.80	01.20	01.60	01.99	02.39	02.79	03.19	03.59
0.1	03.98	04.38	04.78	05.17	05.57	05.96	06.36	06.75	07.14	07.53
0.2	07.93	08.32	08.71	09.10	09.48	09.87	10.26	10.64	11.03	11.41
0.3	11.79	12.17	12.55	12.93	13.31	13.68	14.06	14.43	14.80	15.17
0.4	15.54	15.91	16.28	16.64	17.00	17.36	17.72	18.08	18.44	18.79
0.5	19.15	19.50	19.85	20.19	20.54	20.88	21.23	21.57	21.90	22.24
0.6	22.57	22.91	23.24	23.57	23.89	24.22	24.54	24.86	25.17	25.49
0.7	25.80	26.11	26.42	26.73	27.04	27.34	27.64	27.94	28.23	28.52
0.8	28.81	29.10	29.39	29.67	29.95	30.23	30.51	30.78	31.06	31.33
0.9	31.59	31.86	32.12	32.38	32.64	32.90	33.15	33.40	33.65	33.89
1.0	34.13	34.38	34.61	34.85	35.08	35.31	35.54	35.77	35.99	36.21
1.1	36.43	36.65	36.86	37.08	37.29	37.49	37.70	37.90	38.10	38.30
1.2	38.49	38.69	38.88	39.07	39.25	39.44	39.62	39.80	39.97	40.15
1.3	40.32	40.49	40.66	40.82	40.99	41.15	41.31	41.47	41.62	41.77
1.4	41.92	42.07	42.22	42.36	42.51	42.65	42.79	42.92	43.06	43.19
1.5	43.32	43.45	43.57	43.70	43.83	43.94	44.06	44.18	44.29	44.41
1.6	44.52	44.63	44.74	44.84	44.95	45.05	45.15	45.25	45.35	45.45
1.7	45.54	45.64	45.73	45.82	45.91	45.99	46.08	46.16	46.25	46.33
1.8	46.41	46.49	46.56	46.64	46.71	46.78	46.86	46.93	46.99	47.06
1.9	47.13	47.19	47.26	47.32	47.38	47.44	47.50	47.56	47.61	47.67
2.0	47.72	47.78	47.83	47.88	47.93	47.98	48.03	48.08	48.12	48.17
2.1	48.21	48.26	48.30	48.34	48.38	48.42	48.46	48.50	48.54	48.57
2.2	48.61	48.64	48.68	48.71	48.75	48.78	48.81	48.84	48.87	48.90
2.3	48.93	48.96	48.98	49.01	49.04	49.06	49.09	49.11	49.13	49.16
2.4	49.18	49.20	49.22	49.25	49.27	49.29	49.31	49.32	49.34	49.36
2.5	49.38	49.40	49.41	49.43	49.45	49.46	49.48	49.49	49.51	49.52
2.6	49.53	49.55	49.56	49.57	49.59	49.60	49.61	49.62	49.63	49.64
2.7	49.65	49.66	49.67	49.68	49.69	49.70	49.71	49.72	49.73	49.74
2.8	49.74	49.75	49.76	49.77	49.77	49.78	49.78	49.79	49.80	49.81
2.9	49.81	49.82	49.82	49.83	49.84	49.84	49.85	49.85	49.86	49.86
3.0	49.865									
3.5	49.97674									
5.0	49.99997									

The Normal Distribution Curve 89

* * *

40.32%

---

12. What percent of the cases would fall between the mean and 2.22 standard deviation units? _____.

* * *

48.68%

---

13. Table 1 represents values for ½ of the normal curve.

    Plate 35

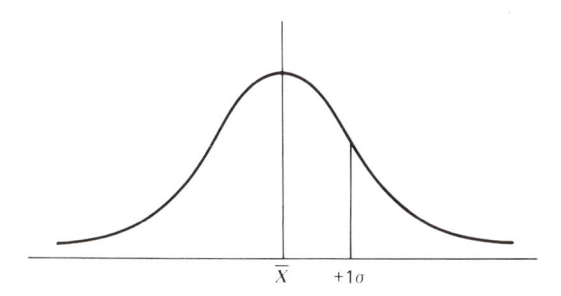

    What percent of the cases fall between the mean and 1.0 standard deviation unit? _____.

* * *

34.13%

---

14. When using Table 1 we must remember where we are in relation to the mean and how we wish to state our results.

    What percentage of the cases of the *whole group* of scores fall below +1.0σ? _____.

* * *

50.0 + 34.13 = 84.13%

90 Using Statistics in Teaching Physical Education

15. Remember the mean is the midpoint of the group of scores and 50% will always represent $\frac{1}{2}$ of the group. The table value must either be added to, or subtracted from, 50% in order to relate the portion to the whole group of scores.

    What percentage of the cases of the *whole group* of scores fall above $+1.0\sigma$? _____.

    * * *

    $50.0 - 34.13 = 15.87\%$

16. Plate 36

    Complete the baseline markings for the left side of the normal curve.

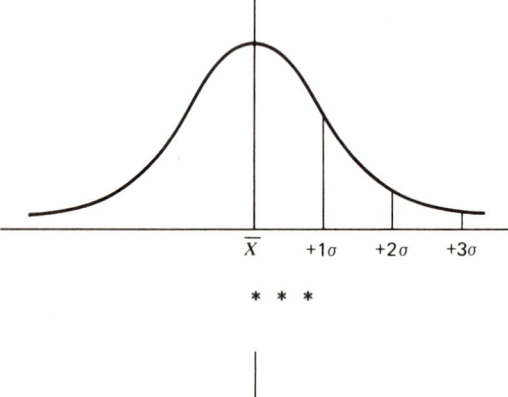

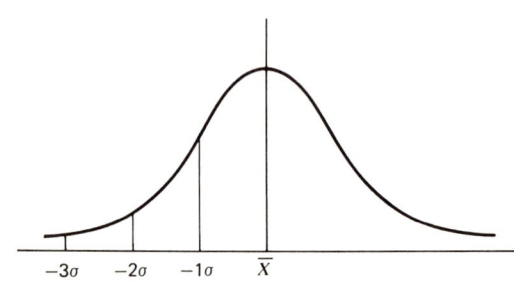

17. The percentage of scores for any area under the normal curve may be obtained from Table 1 by finding the percentage at any given two points and calculating the difference.

    For example, if we wish to know the percentage of scores that fall between 1.0σ and 2.0σ we find the table values for 1.0 (34.13) and 2.0 (47.72) and find the arithmetic difference 13.59.

What percentage of the scores fall between 1.68 and .85 standard deviation units?

* * *

$$45.35 - 30.23 = 15.12\%$$

---

18. Demonstrate this area on the normal curve by shading the appropriate area.

    Plate 37

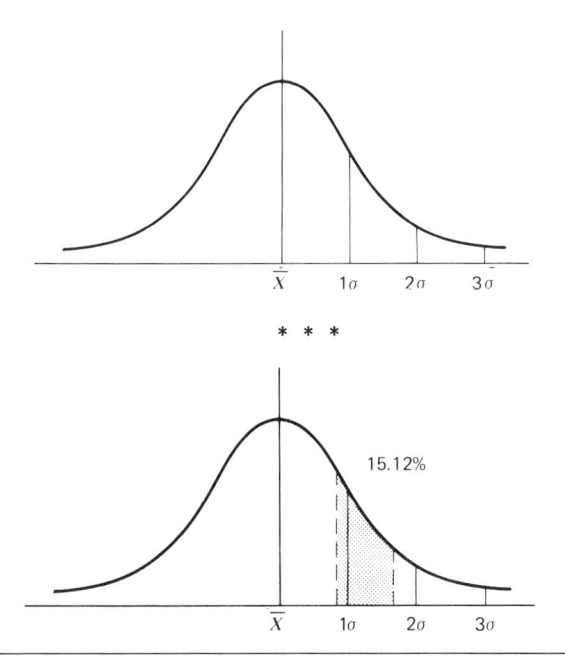

* * *

19. What percentage of the scores are contained between -1σ and $+1\sigma$?
    _____%.

* * *

68.26
(34.13 + 34.13)

20. What percentage of scores would be included between -3σ and $+3\sigma$? _____ %.

* * *

99.73%
(49.865 + 49.865)

21. You will note that the normal curve never does touch the base line. What percent of the cases would fall beyond $+3\sigma$ and -3σ? _____ .

* * *

.27% or .0027
.0027, when dealing with number of people, is insignificant.

22. The normal distribution is a mathematically derived curve. The properties of the curve are very useful to the practitioner because frequency distributions of many sets of data in physical education resemble the _____ curve.

* * *

normal

23. We learned earlier that if a student obtained a score on a skill test of 20, the score told us very little. By calculating the mean of the distribution, we could then know whether the score of 20 was above or below average. By adding the variability measure (σ) we could tell approximately how far above or below the mean the score of 20 was. Now, by applying what we know about the normal curve we can tell exactly where the score falls in relation to the whole group of scores.

If a raw score $X = 20$, the mean $\overline{X} = 30$, and the standard deviation $\sigma = 5$, how many standard deviation units below the mean would the score of 20 be? _____ .

* * *

2.0
(if you're not sure why, look at frame 24)

24. This can be shown graphically:

    Plate 38

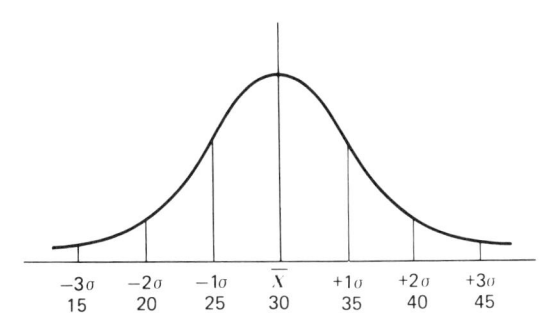

    ```
         -3σ   -2σ   -1σ    X̄    +1σ   +2σ   +3σ
          15    20    25    30    35    40    45
    ```

    The standard deviation is _____.

    * * *

    5

---

25. What percentage of the students in Plate 38 had scores falling between 25 and 35? _____ %.

    * * *

    68.26%

---

26. What percentage of the students in Plate 38 had scores falling between 35 and 40 points? _____ %.

    * * *

    13.59%

---

27. If there were 76 students tested, how many students received scores between 35 and 40 points? _____ %.

    * * *

    13.59% × 76 = 10.33 students

94 Using Statistics in Teaching Physical Education

28. What we did in Frame 23 is called calculating a z score. Formula 8 is used to calculate the z score.

    Formula 8

    $$z = \frac{X - \overline{X}}{\sigma}$$

    Nothing is new in this formula and we can see that we are merely finding the difference between any given raw score and the mean and dividing that difference by the standard deviation.

    Using Formula 8 and the data from Frame 23 ($X = 20, \overline{X} = 30, \sigma = 5$), what is the z score?

    $$z = \frac{X - \overline{X}}{\sigma} = \underline{}$$

    * * *

    $$-2.0$$

    Note. The negative sign indicates that the score is below the mean.

29. The z score then is defined as the number of standard deviation units any given score is from the mean. Assume we measure 45 high school girls on basketball free throw shooting (25 trials). The mean is 9.48 and the standard deviation is 4.6. Pat made 11 out of 25 shots. What is her z score?

    $$z = \frac{X - \overline{X}}{\sigma} \qquad z = \underline{}$$

    * * *

    $$z = .33$$

30. Was Pat's score above the mean or below it? _____.

    * * *

    above

31. This z score is the value used in Table 1 and found in the left hand margin. Using Table 1, what percentage of students fell between the mean and Pat's z score of .33? _____.

* * *

12.93%

32. Since this is a percent, we have to multiply this tabled value by the total number who took the test to find the number of students represented by this portion of the curve.

    In our example (Frame 29) we had 45 girls. How many girls had scores between the mean and Pat's score? _____.

* * *

$45 \times 12.93\% = 5.8$ girls

33. How many girls had scores below Pat's? (Remember, $\frac{1}{2}$ of the scores are to the left of this mean in the normal curve.)

* * *

$22.5 + 5.8 = 28.3$ girls

34. How many girls had scores above Pat's?

* * *

$22.5 - 5.8 = 16.7$ girls

35. When we use z scores, any value above the mean is positive and any value below the mean is negative. A z score for the mean then would be _____.

* * *

zero

96   Using Statistics in Teaching Physical Education

36. Since the *z* score for the mean equals zero, half the *z* scores will have negative values. This is very cumbersome to work with, so three other scales have been developed that use a zero point on the left side of the normal curve, thereby eliminating negative scores.

Negative scale scores can be eliminated by moving the zero point to the _____.

* * *

left

37. How far to the left we go to establish the zero point determines the scale we select. The *sigma scale* goes 3.0 deviations, the *Hull scale* goes 3.5 deviations, and the *T scale* goes 5.0 deviations to the left to establish their zero points.

What is the purpose of moving the zero point to the left in the normal curve? _____.

* * *

to eliminate negative scores

38. The knowledge we have about the normal distribution curve allows us to scale score data. In order for traits to follow the normal distribution curve, however, a large number of measurements must be available (usually 30 or more).

What three scales establish their zero points several standard deviations to the left of the mean in the normal curve? _____
_____.

* * *

the sigma, Hull and T scales

39. We learned, remember, that the normal curve is symmetrical, therefore if we go to the left 3.0, 3.5, or 5.0 deviation units we must also go to the right an equal amount.

The Hull scale includes ± _____ deviation units.

* * *

3.5

---

40. The T scale includes ± _____ deviation units.

* * *

5.0

---

41. The sigma scale is similar to z scores in that it includes ± _____ deviations on each side of the normal curve.

* * *

3.0

---

42. Graphically this would be shown as follows:

   Plate 39

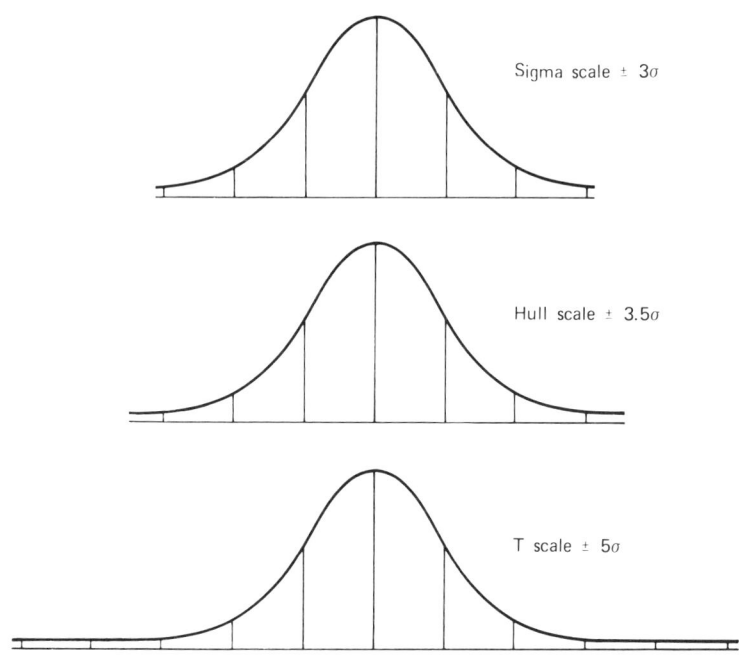

   Sigma scale ± 3σ

   Hull scale ± 3.5σ

   T scale ± 5σ

   Which scale includes the greatest percentage of cases?

98 Using Statistics in Teaching Physical Education

* * *

T scale

---

43. In order to compare the differences of the three scales, use Table 1 to determine the percentage of cases under the normal curve when ±3.0, ±3.5, and ±5.0 deviations from the mean are included.

    sigma =   Hull =   T =

* * *

      sigma   49.865 × 2 = 99.730
      Hull   49.97674 × 2 = 99.95348
      T   49.9999713 × 2 = 99.9999

---

44. Now let's apply these scales. By using Formula 9, 10 or 11 we can convert any set of data into scale scores.

    Formula 9

    $$c_{sigma} = \frac{3.0\sigma}{50}$$

    Formula 10

    $$c_{Hull} = \frac{3.5\sigma}{50}$$

    Formula 11

    $$c_T = \frac{5.0\sigma}{50}$$

    The c stands for a constant change factor. What is the difference in the three formulas? _____.

* * *

deviations used

---

45. Converting sets of raw data into scale scores allows us to manipulate

those scores mathematically, any way we wish. That is, we can add different kinds of quantities. Assume that we wanted to give a badminton test that would test 4 skills and wanted a total score when we finished, so that we could rank the performers on the total badminton test. Let's say we use the following skills: short serve (measured by number of points), a bird tapping test (measured in seconds), the overhead clear (number of points), and a subjective measure of playing ability. It would be unjustified to add these different kinds of quantities to get a total ability score. By scale scoring each component, however, we can then be justified in adding the four component scale scores to determine a final test score. There are many other situations where you may wish to utilize the scale scoring technique. We shall return to this technique when we examine grading systems.

Thus, in addition to eliminating negative signs, converting raw scores to scale scores allows us to do what? _____

_____.

* * *

combine unlike quantities

---

46. The particular scale selected is arbitrary and is left up to the individual teacher. All three scales are frequently used in physical education. The T scale is probably used more frequently in research since it has a greater chance of discriminating between the students on the extreme ends of the range of skills.

    However, scale values are not interchangeable. Therefore, even though the scale selected is optional, a teacher should be consistent and use the selected scale all the time.

    The scale selected _____ (is, is not) optional.

    * * *

    is

---

47. In order to convert a set of raw scores into scale scores we need: the mean, the standard deviation and a selected scale (Formula 9, 10 or 11).

100 Using Statistics in Teaching Physical Education

In addition to the selected scale what else do we need (use symbols) to convert raw scores to scale scores? _____.

* * *

$\bar{X}, \sigma$

---

48. Although the zero point varies, depending on the scale selected, the curve is still symmetrical. All three scales run from 0 to 100. Therefore, the mean for all three scales would be _____.

* * *

50

---

49. There are five steps to computing scale scores:
    1. Select one of the three scales.
    2. Select the appropriate Formula (9, 10 or 11).
    3. Make a list or column of numbers from 0 to 100.
    4. Opposite the 50, place the raw score mean.
    5. Consecutively add and subtract the constant (c) to the raw score mean, once for each number on the scale.

    There are _____ steps in computing scale scores.

* * *

5

---

50. Assume the following data for a group of high school boys on a tennis serve test. We wish to convert these raw scores to scale scores so that we can use the test as part of a grade in physical education.

    We shall use the Hull scale $\bar{X} = 30$, $\sigma = 7.2$
    Step 1: Hull scale
    Step 2: Use Formula 10 $c_{\text{Hull}} = \dfrac{3.5 \times 7.2}{50} = .5$
    Step 3: Make a column of numbers from 0 to 100
    Step 4: Place $\bar{X}$ at the 50
    Step 5: Consecutively add and subtract constant ($c = .5$) to mean

Plate 40

Scale Score	Raw Score
100	
*	
*	
60	35
59	34.5
58	34
57	33.5
56	33
55	32.5
54	32
53	31.5
52	31
51	30.5
50	30
49	29.5
48	29
47	28.5
46	28
45	27.5
44	27

What would the Hull scale score be for the following raw scores:
27 (   ), 29 (   ), 34 (   )

* * *

27 (44), 29 (48), 34 (58)

---

51. Now see if you can remember the 5 steps used to construct a set of scale scores.

   Step 1

   Step 2

   Step 3

   Step 4

   Step 5

Step 1 Select scale
Step 2 Compute c
Step 3 Make a column 0–100
Step 4 Place $\bar{X}$ at 50 on the scale
Step 5 Consecutively add and subtract c to $\bar{X}$

---

52. Converting raw scores to scale scores is a valuable technique for the physical educator because many unlike quantities can be combined (time, errors, distance, weight, etc.) using this technique.

    In order to combine unlike quantities, we convert raw scores to _____ _____.

* * *

scale scores

EXERCISES FOR SET 6

1. In the normal distribution curve, what is the relationship of the mean, median and mode?
2. Calculate z scores for the following raw scores when the $\bar{X}=61.2$ and $\sigma=4.6$.

   Formula 8 $z = \dfrac{X - \bar{X}}{\sigma}$

   a. 56.0
   b. 58.2
   c. 64.6
3. Using Table 1, find the percentage of cases that fall between:
   a. mean and 1.0 deviation units
   b. mean and .67 deviation units
   c. .72 and 2.30 deviation units
   d. .08 and 1.37 deviation units
4. Using Table 1, find the number of people out of 200 that would fall under the normal distribution curve between:
   a. mean and 1.0 deviation units

b. .65 and 1.23 deviation units
c. plus and minus 1.0 deviation units
d. minus .37 and plus 1.2 deviation units
5. Convert the following set of raw scores (weights of seven year old boys) into T scale scores.

T Scale Score	Raw Score
	52
	59
	52
	59
	62
	48
	52
	55
	53
	42
	52
	45
	47
	48

$\bar{X} = 51.86$
$\sigma = 5.4$

Turn to page 104 for answers.

ANSWERS FOR SET 6 EXERCISES

1. They are the same.

2. a. -1.13 b. $-.65$ c. .74
3. a. 34.13   b. 24.86   c. 22.51   d. 38.28
4. a. 68.26   b. 29.70   c. 136.52   d. 105.84

5.

T Scale Score	Raw Score
50	52
63	59
50	52
63	59
69	62
43	48
50	52
56	55
52	53
32	42
50	52
37	45
41	47
43	48

SET 7
The Mean and Standard Deviation with Grouped Data

Units 3, 4 and 5 dealt with ungrouped data. You learned how to calculate measures of central tendency, variability and correlation when the quantity of data was relatively small. With larger amounts of data, the principles you have learned about measures of central tendency, variability and correlation still hold true, but we can use more efficient methods of calculation.

OBJECTIVES

After completion of this set you will be able to:
1. Establish a frequency table for a large number of scores.
2. Calculate the mean using Formula 12.
3. Calculate the standard deviation using Formula 13.

---

1. The mean, as we have already learned, is defined as the arithmetic average of the set of scores.

    When we have a large number of scores in a set of data (30 or more), the mean is easier to calculate if the scores are grouped into intervals.

    Raw scores, when the amount of data is large, are clumped together into categories for analyses called _____ .

intervals

---

2. The symbol used to represent the interval is the lower case *i*. The size of the interval is arbitrary. Intervals are usually set up by using an odd number (e.g., 3, 5, 7, 9) to ease calculation; however, the interval range can be any number.

   To indicate the interval in a distribution of grouped data what symbol is used? _____ .

   * * *

   i

---

3. Assume we have the following nine scores obtained from a beginning bowling class (with grouped data we need 30 scores or more—we're just using nine as a simple example):

   Plate 41

   88, 99, 89, 95, 94, 92, 97, 98, 88

   If we want to group these nine scores into categories or intervals, we first need to determine the range of the scores.

   Formula 2

   $$\text{Range} = \text{highest} - \text{lowest} + 1$$

   Find the range of the nine numbers.

   * * *

   $$99 - 88 + 1 = 12$$

---

4. We wish to group the nine numbers into categories or intervals that will contain an odd number of scores. If we divide the range by 2 or 3

The Mean and Standard Deviation with Grouped Data 109

we get an even number (6 or 4). If we divide 12 by 4 = 3 we will have four intervals containing three numbers each. Using scores in Plate 41, place a tally mark for each score in the appropriate interval.

Plate 42

i	tally
97–99	
94–96	
91–93	
88–90	

* * *

i	tally
97–99	111
94–96	11
91–93	1
88–90	111

5. The resulting tally is the frequency for each interval, that is, there are three scores in the interval 97–99, two in the interval 94–96, etc. The f or frequency column added to the table merely summarizes the tallies.

Plate 43

i	tally	f
97–99	111	3
94–96	11	2
91–93	1	1
88–90	111	3

How many scores were there in the interval 88–90? _____.

* * *

3

6. We will discuss in more detail how to set up the intervals later.

   Remember, the procedure we are now learning is for a large set of data ($N > 30$). Example numbers are kept as small as possible so the concept can be understood. It is best to have between 9 and 18 intervals in a frequency distribution.

   The number of intervals you have is dependent on the interval size and the _____ of scores.

   * * *

   range

---

7. In Plate 44, there are 40 scores obtained on a soccer dribbling test for high school boys.

   Plate 44

7	12	14	33	18
19	20	21	22	25
26	27	29	16	19
10	13	30	23	18
20	20	21	23	24
11	28	15	16	19
20	13	15	17	25
27	21	22	17	24

   What is the range? _____.

   * * *

   $33 - 7 + 1 = 27$

---

8. The range is 27. The next procedure is to determine what the class interval will be. We divide 27 by some number that will give us

between 9 and 18 class intervals and preferably an odd number of steps or score values within the interval.

What number would you divide the range by? _____.

* * *

3

---

9. By dividing the range 27 by 3, we will have nine class intervals with three numbers or score values in each interval. To begin setting up the frequency distribution, start with an interval that will include the highest number in your set of data. For the data in Plate 44 this number is: _____.

* * *

33

---

10. The top interval, then, must include the number 33. Likewise, the lowest interval must include the lowest or smallest number in our distribution, which is _____.

* * *

7

---

11. Set up the interval column by starting with the top interval as shown. Decrease the intervals by three until you have an interval that includes the lowest score 7.

Plate 45

i
31–33
28–30

112 Using Statistics in Teaching Physical Education

* * *

i
31–33
28–30
25–27
22–24
19–21
16–18
13–15
10–12
7– 9

12. It is a good idea to check the column of numbers since it is easy to make a mistake at this point. To check, start at the bottom of each column in i and progressively add the step interval to each number.

The symbol for the interval is i. Remember that i equals the number of score values represented in the interval. In this case $i =$ _____.

* * *

3

13. Look at the top three intervals.

   Plate 46

i
31–33
28–30
25–27

In our example the variable is discrete; however, if it were continuous we would have to know the exact limits of the interval steps. The exact limits of the intervals in Plate 44 are:

Plate 47

i
30.5–33.4
27.5–30.4
24.5–27.4

Find the exact intervals for the next three intervals of descending value.

Plate 48

i	exact value
22–24	
19–21	
16–18	

* * *

i	exact value
22–24	21.5–24.4
19–21	18.5–21.4
16–18	15.5–18.4

14. Exact intervals are needed primarily when using continuous variables. Knowledge of exact values also is used to calculate percentiles, which we will learn later.

Exact intervals are used primarily when you have _____ variables.

* * *

continuous

15. If we had the intervals as shown below, indicate the tally for each of the following numbers:

$$27.2, \quad 31.6, \quad 27.9, \quad 30.4, \quad 29.2$$

Plate 49

i	tally
31–33	
28–30	
25–27	

* * *

i	tally
31–33	1
28–30	111
25–27	1

16. Using the soccer scores in Plate 44 (Frame 7), tally the raw scores in the frequency table as constructed in Frame 11. Also include an f column which summarizes the tallies.

i	tally	f

The Mean and Standard Deviation with Grouped Data 115

* * *

i	tally	f
31–33	1	1
28–30	111	3
25–27	̶I̶I̶I̶I̶	5
22–24	̶I̶I̶I̶I̶ 1	6
19–21	̶I̶I̶I̶I̶ ̶I̶I̶I̶I̶	10
16–18	̶I̶I̶I̶I̶ 1	6
13–15	̶I̶I̶I̶I̶	5
10–12	111	3
7–9	1	1

17. The next step in setting up the frequency table is to estimate in which interval the mean will be. By looking at the distribution in the answer of Frame 16, within which interval would you suspect the mean to be? _____.

* * *

the mean is probably in the interval 19–21 because the scores are fairly equally distributed and there are the greatest frequency of scores in this interval

18. The mean can be estimated as being within any class interval in the distribution. By selecting an interval below that interval where you really believe the mean will be, you can eliminate negative numbers in future calculations.

Selecting a mean that is below our real estimate eliminates _____ _____ in calculations.

* * *

negative numbers

19. The midpoint score within the estimated interval is the estimated or guessed mean, thus the advantage of having an odd number of scores in each interval.

The midpoint of the interval 19–21 is _____.

* * *

20

---

20. The symbol to be used for the estimated mean is $E\overline{X}$. The estimated mean is the _____ of any class interval. The symbol for the estimated mean is _____.

* * *

middle score, $E\overline{X}$

---

21. The frequency table is completed by adding three additional columns. These additional columns are based on the estimated mean ($E\overline{X}$) and measure the deviation of each interval from the estimated mean interval (d), the distance of each interval away from the $E\overline{X}$ times the frequency of scores within each interval (fd), and the product of $d \cdot fd$ or fd^2. The following columns are needed for the frequency table.

Plate 50

| i | tally | f | d | fd | fd^2 |

What does d represent? _____

* * *

the distance each interval is away
from the estimated mean interval

---

22. From the frequency distribution table we can obtain Σfd and Σfd^2. With these two quantities the actual mean and the standard deviation can be calculated.

The symbol used to represent the sum of the products of the scores within an interval and the distance of that interval away from the estimated mean is _____.

* * *

Σfd

---

23. Plate 51

i	f	d
31–33	1	4
28–30	3	3
25–27	5	2
22–24	6	1
$E\overline{X}$ 19–21	10	0
16–18	6	−1
13–15	5	−2
10–12	3	−3
7– 9	1	−4

The estimated mean in Plate 51 is _____. Therefore, the value of d for the estimated mean is _____.

* * *

20, 0
(it is zero deviations away from itself)

---

24. In Plate 51, there are how many intervals above and below the estimated mean? _____.

* * *

4 above and 4 below

118 Using Statistics in Teaching Physical Education

25. It is not necessary, however, to have the same number of intervals above and below the $E\overline{X}$. Now we will complete the fd column by simply multiplying f times d noting the signs.

Plate 52

i	f	d	fd
31–33	1	4	4
28–30	3	3	9
25–27	5	2	10
22–24	6	1	6
$E\overline{X}$ 19–21	10	0	0
16–18	6	−1	−6
13–15	5	−2	−10
10–12	3	−3	−9
7– 9	1	−4	−4
			$\Sigma fd=$

To find the Σfd, the column fd must be added by observing the signs. $\Sigma fd=$ _____ .

* * *

$$29+(-29)=0$$

26. The final step in completing the frequency table is to find the fd^2 column. This is done by multiplying the d column by the fd column, observing the signs.

Plate 53

i	f	d	fd	fd^2
31–33	1	4	4	16
28–30	3	3	9	27
25–27	5	2	10	20
22–24	6	1	6	6
$E\overline{X}$ 19–21	10	0	0	0
16–18	6	−1	−6	6
13–15	5	−2	−10	20
10–12	3	−3	−9	27
7– 9	1	−4	−4	16
			$\Sigma fd=$	$\Sigma fd^2=$

To find the Σfd^2 add the column fd^2. All numbers in this column should be positive. What is $\Sigma fd^2 = $ _____ .

* * *

138

---

27. The distribution table is now completed and we have all the information necessary to calculate the mean and standard deviation.

    When the data is grouped the mean is found by Formula 12.

    Formula 12

    $$\overline{X} = E\overline{X} + \left(\frac{\Sigma fd}{N} \cdot i\right)$$

    Substitute information from our problem (Plate 53) into Formula 12. (Don't solve it yet.)

    * * *

    $$\overline{X} = 20 + \left(\frac{0}{40} \cdot 3\right)$$

---

28. Now solve the equation for $\overline{X}$. _____ .

    * * *

    $$\overline{X} = 20$$

---

29. In the previous problem was the calculated mean the same or different than the estimated mean? _____ .

120 Using Statistics in Teaching Physical Education

* * *

same
(this happened in this example using small numbers and a balanced distribution of scores; however, it is unusual for the actual mean of a large number of scores to be identical to the estimated mean)

---

30. Setting up the distribution table may seem tedious at first; however, the procedure is not difficult. It is mainly mechanical and there would be no additional steps even though there might be five times as many raw scores (i.e., $N = 200$).

The standard deviation also is found from information in the distribution table using Formula 13.

Formula 13

$$\sigma = i\sqrt{\frac{\Sigma fd^2}{N} - \left(\frac{\Sigma fd}{N}\right)^2}$$

Substitute information from Plates 52 and 53 into Formula 13. (Don't solve it yet.)

* * *

$$\sigma = 3\sqrt{\frac{138}{40} - \left(\frac{0}{40}\right)^2}$$

---

31. Now solve the equation for σ.

$$\sigma = 5.57$$

---

32. You should now be able to properly set up a frequency table and calculate the $\overline{X}$ and σ for grouped data.

    To review, the procedures are:
    1. Find the range.
    2. Select a step interval (between 9 and 18).
    3. Set up the intervals to include top and bottom scores.
    4. Tally the scores.
    5. Select an estimated mean.
    6. Determine f, fd and fd^2 columns.
    7. Find Σfd and Σfd^2.
    8. Apply Formulas 12 and 13 to calculate the $\overline{X}$ and σ.

    These procedures are followed to determine the $\overline{X}$ and σ of _____ data.

    * * *

    grouped

EXERCISES FOR SET 7

1. Scores for a medicine ball put for 50 high school boys are listed. Formulate a frequency distribution table and determine:

    a. range
    b. Σfd
    c. Σfd^2
    d. $\overline{X}$
    e. σ

    (Use Frame 32 for assistance, if necessary.)

122 Using Statistics in Teaching Physical Education

Note. In order to be able to check your work, use a step interval of 3, a top interval of 51–53, and an $E\bar{X}$ of 34.

40	44	23	21	20
47	47	46	42	45
39	52	46	41	16
47	47	49	42	25
44	38	22	43	35
21	26	32	22	29
30	35	40	43	27
28	38	48	24	34
48	44	39	37	35
44	40	35	18	20

i	tally	f	d	fd	fd^2

Formula 12

$$\bar{X} = E\bar{X} + \left(\frac{\Sigma fd}{N} \cdot i\right)$$

Formula 13

$$\sigma = i\sqrt{\frac{\Sigma fd^2}{N} - \left(\frac{\Sigma fd}{N}\right)^2}$$

2. Scores for 40 high school girls on an obstacle run are listed below. Formulate a frequency distribution table and determine:
   a. the range
   b. Σfd
   c. Σfd^2
   d. $\bar{X}$
   e. σ

   (Use Frame 37 for assistance, if necessary.

   Note. Select an appropriate interval size and any estimated mean.

34.1	37.8	73.0	40.5	55.8
70.0	39.0	35.3	42.5	35.5
41.5	54.3	34.3	37.0	47.2
38.5	46.8	35.2	78.0	35.8
37.0	34.0	48.2	44.8	43.2
35.7	68.2	52.5	57.6	49.6
39.2	43.8	42.1	57.2	54.5
39.6	36.7	39.9	37.2	45.8

i	tally	f	d	fd	fd^2

Formula 12

$$\bar{X} = E\bar{X} + \left(\frac{\Sigma fd}{N} \cdot i\right)$$

Formula 13

$$\sigma = i\sqrt{\frac{\Sigma fd^2}{N} - \left(\frac{\Sigma fd}{N}\right)^2}$$

ANSWERS FOR SET 7 EXERCISES

1. a. range = 37
   b. $\Sigma fd = 29$
   c. $\Sigma fd^2 = 551$
   d. $\bar{X} = 35.74$
   e. $\sigma = 9.80$

2. a. range = 45
   b. $\Sigma fd = 29$ ⎫ These two numbers vary, depending on the selected interval size and estimated mean.
   c. $\Sigma fd^2 = 209$ ⎭
   d. $\bar{X} = 46.63$ ⎫ The $\bar{X}$ and σ should be approximately the same as these values regardless of the selected interval size and estimated mean.
   e. $\sigma = 10.84$ ⎭

SET 8
Correlation with Grouped Data

Set 5 provided material necessary for calculation of correlation coefficients for ungrouped data. Often we need to determine test validity, reliability and objectivity, and also often wish to determine relationships among various variables when the N is large.

When we have a large number of pairs of scores and wish to calculate a correlation coefficient, we use the grouped data technique called the scattergram. Principles from Set 6 and Set 7 carry into this unit.

OBJECTIVES

After completion of this set you must be able to:

1. Starting with pairs of raw scores, compute a correlation coefficient using the scattergram method and Formula 14.

---

1. The scattergram technique is used to calculate a correlation coefficient when the number of pairs of scores is _____ .

* * *

large

2. When we have a large number of pairs of scores, the _____ technique is more efficient than using an ungrouped technique.

* * *

scattergram

---

3. The term "a large number of pairs of scores" is rather vague. The size of the scores and the availability of a calculator enter into the decision as to what number of scores becomes a "large number." It is generally safe to say that any time you have over 50 pairs of scores you should use the grouped technique for calculating correlations. The scattergram should be used any time there are around _____ or more pairs of scores.

* * *

50

---

4. The scattergram is merely a matrix, or a group of lines, arranged to make the tabulation of data easier. The size of the matrix varies, depending on the number of intervals or groups of scores we will have with each variable.

The physical layout of a scattergram is called a _____ .

* * *

matrix

---

5. When we use the grouped data technique to determine a correlation coefficient, we establish frequency tables just as we did in Set 7. With a correlation, however, we have two sets of scores; therefore, we work with two frequency tables simultaneously.

Calculation of a correlation coefficient with grouped data involves establishing how many frequency tables?

Correlation with Grouped Data 131

* * *

two

---

6. Plate 54 represents the matrix used in calculating a correlation coefficient with grouped data. We use the box in the upper left hand corner of the matrix to indicate which variable is represented by the horizontal plane and which is represented by the vertical plane.

Plate 54

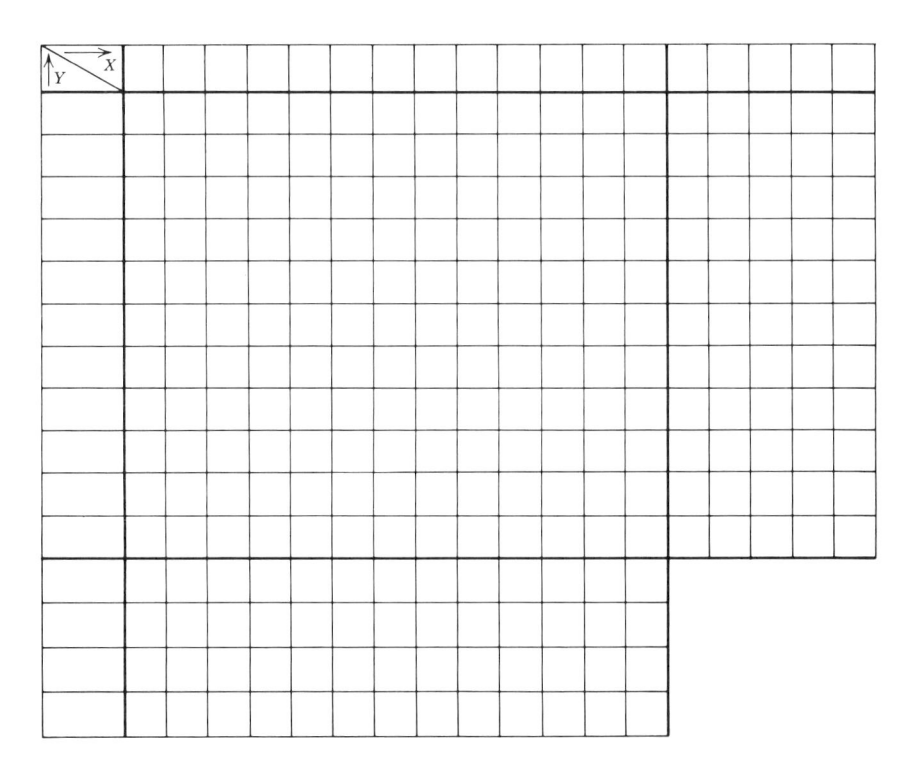

All intervals, tallies, deviations and sums for the X variable will be found by the _____ plane.

* * *

horizontal

7. On which plane would we find all intervals, tallies, deviations and sums for the Y variable? _____.

* * *

on the vertical plane

8. To illustrate the calculation procedures used with the scattergram technique, the following data will be used.

Plate 55
Scores received on a badminton long serve test and a short serve test.

long serve (X)	short serve (Y)	long	short
14	4	42	33
30	22	42	30
11	2	38	28
34	31	21	3
38	23	29	21
15	6	38	12
46	28	29	24
19	10	25	16
23	14	17	16
19	5	32	20
12	14	44	29
30	17	33	26
27	22	31	17
36	24	21	12
30	19	17	8
36	26	27	20
40	29	18	13
46	32	17	11
24	15	13	4
44	31	25	8
43	29	29	13
32	28	28	20
36	19	10	5
42	27	23	23
36	12	19	21

Which variable is represented by X? _____.

* * *

long serve

---

9. Find the range of scores for the variables X and Y in Plate 55. _____
   _____.

* * *

range of $X = 37$, range of $Y = 32$

---

10. To establish a step interval of three with the appropriate number of intervals desired, you would divide the ranges by what number? _____
    _____.

* * *

probably by 12

---

11. If we divide both ranges by 12, we will have a step interval (i) of three for both variables with 11 or 12 intervals or groups of scores.

    When setting up the intervals for both variables the arrows in the upper left hand box represent the direction, in ascending order, for each variable's intervals.

    The interval that would contain the highest score for the X variable would appear where—in the far right box, or the far left box? _____
    _____.

* * *

the far right box

---

12. Plate 56 shows the scattergram matrix with the class intervals established and the table headings labeled. The empty column on the right will be considered later.

Using Statistics in Teaching Physical Education

Plate 56

$\vec{X}$ / Y	10 12	13 15	16 18	19 21	22 24	25 27	28 30	31 33	34 36	37 39	40 42	43 45	46 48	f_y	d_y	fd_y	fd_y^2
31-33																	
28-30																	
25-27																	
22-24																	
19-21																	
16-18																	
13-15																	
10-12																	
7-9																	
4-6																	
1-3																	
f_x																	
d_x																	
fd_x																	
fd_x^2																	

Summation of which column would represent N? _____ (symbol)

* * *

Σf_x or Σf_y

---

13. The object of establishing the frequency table in Set 7 was to find Σfd and Σfd^2. This is also the purpose of the scattergram. Here, however, we are finding the Σfd and Σfd^2 for two sets of scores simultaneously. To differentiate between the means, sums and standard deviations of the two sets of variables we simply use a subscript (i.e., fd_x, $\bar{X}_y$, or σ_x).

The symbol for the sum of the products of the deviations away from the mean and the frequency within each interval for the Y variable would be _____.

Correlation with Grouped Data 135

* * *

$$\Sigma f d_y$$

---

14. The symbol for the standard deviation of the Y variable would be _____ .

* * *

σ_y

---

15. However, N would not have a subscript. Can you guess why not? _____ .

* * *

because N represents the number of pairs of scores

---

16. Now we are ready to tally the scores. This procedure is similar to establishing the frequency table except that one tally mark represents a *pair* of scores. Frame 8, Plate 55, lists the pairs of raw scores. The first column is variable X and the second is variable Y. The first pair of numbers is 14 and 4. Since 14 represents the X variable, which is *horizontal*, we proceed in the direction of the X arrow until we find the interval that includes the score 14. We then traverse vertically in the direction of the Y arrow until we find the vertical interval that includes the score 4.

Within this box we enter one tally. This is repeated until all pairs of scores are entered in the matrix. Make the tally marks small in one corner of the box since other numbers will also be entered within the boxes.

Use Plate 56 to tally the 50 pairs of badminton serve scores, then compare your results with Plate 57 in Frame 17.

---

17. Plate 57 shows the scattergram with the tallies. The next step is to duplicate the steps learned in developing the frequency table. That is,

136 Using Statistics in Teaching Physical Education

estimate the mean and find f, d, fd, fd^2 for each of the variables separately. Plate 57 is partially completed. Complete Plate 57 so that you can obtain the Σfd_x, Σfd_x^2, Σfd_y, Σfd_y^2.

Hint. Draw heavy lines bordering the estimated mean interval for both variables. The estimated mean intervals are noted by an asterisk.

Plate 57

	10 12	13 15	16 18	19 21	22 24	25 27	28 30	31 33	34 36	37 39	40 42	43 45	46 48	f_y	d_y	fd_y	fd_y^2	Σfm
31-33							1		1	1	1							
28-30						1		1		11	11	1						
25-27						1	1		1									
22-24				1	1	11		1	1					6	2	12	24	
19-21				1		1	111	1	1					7	1	7	7	
16-18			1		1	1	1							4	0	0	0	0
13-15		1		1	11		1							5	-1	-5	5	
10-12			1	11				1	1									
7-9			1			1												
4-6	1	111		1														
1-3	1			1														
f_x			4	5	3	4	7											
d_x				-2	-1	0	1	2	3	4								
fd_x				-10	-3	0	7											
fd_x^2				20	3	0	7											

Find $\Sigma fd_x =$ $\Sigma fd_x^2 =$ $\Sigma fd_y =$ $\Sigma fd_y^2 =$

* * *

$\Sigma fd_x = 42$ $\Sigma fd_x^2 = 604$ $\Sigma fd_y = 25$ $\Sigma fd_y^2 = 443$

18. To confirm that the correct number of tallies has been made, compare the sum of the f_x column and the sum of the f_y column to the original number of paired scores.

   In plate 57, if one were to find the sums of the f_x and f_y columns, he should have $N =$ _____.

   * * *

   50

---

19. The sum of the f_x column should be the same as the sum of the f_y column. Explain why. _____

   _____.

   * * *

   because they are paired scores—each X
   score is paired with a Y score

---

20. We shall now proceed to find the sum of the Σfm column at the far right of the matrix. As you already know, f stands for frequency. The lower case m stands for "moment." The symbol for the product of the frequency and moment would be _____.

   * * *

   fm

---

21. Each box in the matrix has a moment value. The moment is a number that represents the deviation of each *box* away from the *combined estimated mean*. All boxes have moment values regardless of whether they have any tallies in them. We'll see in the next few frames how to calculate the moment.

   What does a moment value represent? _____

   _____.

138 Using Statistics in Teaching Physical Education

* * *

the deviation of each box in the matrix away
from the combined estimated means

---

22. The next few frames illustrate how the moment values are derived. First the matrix is divided into quadrants based on the estimated mean intervals. The upper right and lower left quadrants have positive values. The upper left and lower right quadrant boxes have negative values.

    Plate 58
    Illustrate the quadrants. One sign is indicated. Add the signs for the remaining quadrants.

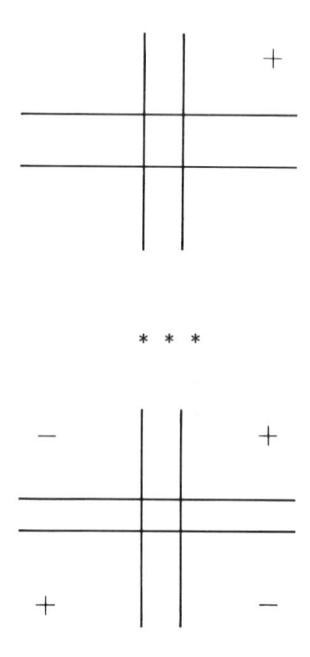

$$\begin{array}{c|c} & + \\ \hline & \end{array}$$

* * *

$$\begin{array}{c|c} - & + \\ \hline + & - \end{array}$$

---

23. Each box is numbered starting with 1, 2, 3, 4 etc., vertically and horizontally as shown in Plate 59 (lower left quadrant). These first deviation number values are then added once for each subsequent deviation from both estimated mean intervals, that is, 3, 6, 9, 12, 15

Correlation with Grouped Data 139

(see upper right quadrant). Another way to find the value of each moment is to multiply the number in the first row and column for each moment box (e.g., $4 \times 5 = 20$).

Plate 59

Y \ X	10 12	13 15	16 18	19 21	22 24	25 27	28 30	31 33	34 36	37 39	40 42	43 45	46 48			
31-33							5	10	15	20	25	30	35			
28-30			-8	-4			4	8	12	16	20	24	28			
25-27			-9	-6	-3		3	6	9	12	15	18	21			
22-24			-6	-4	-2		2	4	6	8	10	12	14			
19-21			-3	-2	-1		1	2	3	4	5	6	7			
16-18																
13-15	5	4	3	2	1											
10-12					2											
7-9					3											
4-6					4			B								
1-3	A				5											

For practice, complete the box numbering for the lower right and lower left quadrants. What are the moment values for the boxes labeled A and B? (Remember the signs). _____.

* * *

A = 25, B = −12

24. We only need to find the moment values for boxes that have tallies.

What is the moment for the box representing the pair of scores 15 and 6? _____.

140 Using Statistics in Teaching Physical Education

* * *

16 (4×4)

---

25. Go back to Plate 57, add lines for the estimated mean intervals, and find the moments for each box with tallies. Place this number in the box. (Keep this number small since one more number needs to go in the box. It is helpful to use a different colored pen or pencil for each number entered in the box).

* * *

Y \ X	10 12	13 15	16 18	19 21	22 24	25 27	28 30	31 33	34 36	37 39	40 42	43 45	46 48	f_y	d_y	fd_y	fd_y^2	Σfm
31-33								1 15 / 15		1 25 / 25	1 30 / 30	1 35 / 35						
28-30							1 8 / 8		1 16 / 16	11 40 / 40	20 48 / 48	11 24 / 28	1 28					
25-27								1 6 1 / 6	9 / 9		1 15 / 15							
22-24				1 -2 / -2	1	11 2 / 4		1 6 / 6	1 8 / 8					6	2	12	24	
19-21			1 -2 / -2		1	111 1 1 / 3	2 1 / 2	1 3 / 3						7	1	7	7	
16-18			1			1	1							4	0	0	0	0
13-15	1 5 / 5	1 3 / 3		11 1 / 2		1 -1 / -1								5	-1	-5	5	
10-12			1 6 11 4 / 6	8				1 -6 / -6	1 -8 / -8									
7-9			1 9 / 9		1													
4-6	1 20 111 16 / 20	48		1 8 / 8														
1-3	1 25 / 25			1 10 / 10														
f_x			4	5	3	4	7											
d_x				-2	-1	0	1	2	3	4								
fd_x				-10	-3	0	7											
fd_x^2				20	3	0	7											

---

26. The next step is to complete the work within the boxes by multiplying the frequency within each box by the moment of the box *noting the signs*. A typical completed box is shown in Plate 60.

Correlation with Grouped Data 141

Plate 60

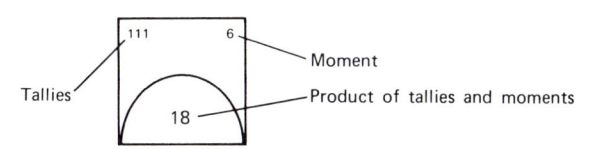

Tallies — 111 / 6
Moment
Product of tallies and moments — 18

Return to Plate 57 and calculate the *fm* for each box having tallies.

* * *

Y \ X	10 12	13 15	16 18	19 21	22 24	25 27	28 30	31 33	34 36	37 39	40 42	43 45	46 48	f_y	d_y	fd_y	fd_y^2	Σfm
31-33									1 / 15 / 15		1 25 / 25 / 30	1 30 / 30	1 35 / 35					
28-30								1 8 / 8		1 16 / 16 / 40	11 20 / 40 / 48	1 24 / 48 / 28	1 28 / 28					
25-27								1 6 / 6 / 9	1 9 / 9		1 15 / 15 / 15							
22-24				1 -2 / -2	1		11 2 / 4		1 6 / 6 / 8	1 8 / 8				6	2	12	24	
19-21			1 -2 / -2		1	111 1 / 3 / 3	1 2 / 2 / 3	1 3 / 3						7	1	7	7	
16-18			1	1	1	1								4	0	0	0	0
13-15	1 5 / 5	1 3 / 3	11 1 / 2 / 2	1 -1 / -1										5	-1	-5	5	
10-12		1 6 / 6	11 4 / 8 / 8					1 -6 / -6 / -6	1 -8 / -8 / -8									
7-9		1 9 / 9		1														
4-6	1 20 / 20	111 16 / 48	1 8 / 8															
1-3	1 25 / 25		1 10 / 10															
f_x				4	5	3	4	7										
d_x				-2	-1	0	1	2	3	4								
fd_x				-10	-3	0	7											
fd_x^2				20	3	0	7											

27. What is the *fm* for the three scores in the box for 15 and 6?

* * *

48

28. The Σfm column can now be determined by adding algebraically, horizontally, all the *fm*'s of each box. Note the signs as you add,

142 Using Statistics in Teaching Physical Education

because some numbers will be negative. For example, the fourth horizontal row from the top has the numbers −2, 4, 6, 8 which equal 16.

What is the sum of the fifth row? _____.

* * *

6

---

29. Now that we have obtained all of the sums for each row, we need to find the sum of the Σfm column. Since this is the sum of a column that is made up of sums of rows, we will write this as $\Sigma\Sigma fm$.

The symbol for the sum of the sum of tallies and the moment of the box is _____.

* * *

$\Sigma\Sigma fm$

---

30. Return to Plate 57 and calculate the $\Sigma\Sigma fm$. The $\Sigma\Sigma fm$ equals _____.

Y \ X	10 12	13 15	16 18	19 21	22 24	25 27	28 30	31 33	34 36	37 39	40 42	43 45	46 48	f_y	d_y	fd_y	fd_y^2	Σfm
31–33							1 / 15	1 / 15		1 25 / 25	1 30 / 30	1 35 / 35		4	5	20	100	105
28–30						1 8 / 8	1 8 / 8		1 16 / 16	11 20 / 40	11 24 / 48	1 28 / 28		7	4	28	112	140
25–27						1 6 / 6	1 9 / 9	1 6 / 6		1 15 / 15				3	3	9	27	30
22–24				1 −2 / −2	1	11 2 / 4		1 6 / 6	1 8 / 8					6	2	12	24	16
19–21			1 −2 / −2		1	111 1 / 3	1 2 / 2	1 3 / 3						7	1	7	7	6
16–18			1			1	1							4	0	0	0	0
13–15	1 5 / 5	1 3 / 3		11 1 / 2		1 −1 / −1								5	−1	−5	5	9
10–12			1 6 / 6	11 4 / 8				1 −6 / −6	1 −8 / −8					5	−2	−10	20	0
7–9		1 9 / 9		1										2	−3	−6	18	9
4–6	1 20 / 20	111 16 / 48	1 8 / 8											5	−4	−20	80	76
1–3	1 25 / 25		1 10 / 10											2	−5	−10	50	35
f_x	3	3	4	5	3	4	7	4	5	3	4	3	2	N	25	443	426	
d_x	−5	−4	−3	−2	−1	0	1	2	3	4	5	6	7					
fd_x	−15	−12	−12	−10	−3	0	7	8	15	12	20	18	14	=42				
fd_x^2	75	48	36	20	3	0	7	16	45	48	100	108	98	=604				

Correlation with Grouped Data 143

* * *

$$\Sigma\Sigma fm = 426$$

---

31. The scattergram is now finished. The steps you have completed should make the scattergram constructed in Plate 57 look like Plate 61. (Remember all sums for x are obtained from the horizontal rows and all sums of y are obtained from vertical columns.)

Plate 61

Y \ X	10-12	13-15	16-18	19-21	22-24	25-27	28-30	31-33	34-36	37-39	40-42	43-45	46-48	f_y	d_y	fd_y	fd_y^2	Σfm
31-32								1/15 (15)		1/25 (25)	1/30 (30)	1/35 (35)		4	5	20	100	105
28-30							1/8 (8)		1/16 (16)	16/40 (40)	11/20/48 (48)	11/24/28 (28)		7	4	28	112	140
25-27							1/6 (6)	1/9 (9)		1/15 (15)				3	3	9	27	30
22-24				1/-2 (-2)	1		11/2 (4)	1/6 (6)	1/8 (8)					6	2	12	24	16
19-21			1/-2 (-2)		1		111/1 (3)	2/1 (2)	1/3 (3)					7	1	7	7	6
16-18		1					1	1						4	0	0	0	0
13-15	1/5 (5)		1/3 (3)		11/1 (2)		1/-1 (-1)							5	-1	-5	5	9
10-12			1/6 (6)	11/4 (8)					1/-6 (-6)	1/-8 (-8)				5	-2	-10	20	0
7-9			1/9 (9)	1										2	-3	-6	18	9
4-6	1/20 (20)	111/16 (48)		1/8 (8)										5	-4	-20	80	76
1-3	1/25 (25)		1/10 (10)											2	-5	-10	50	35
f_x	3	3	4	5	3	4	7	4	5	3	4	3	2	N		25	443	426
d_x	-5	-4	-3	-2	-1	0	1	2	3	4	5	6	7					
fd_x	-15	-12	-12	-10	-3	0	7	8	15	12	20	18	14	=42				
fd_x^2	75	48	36	20	3	0	7	16	45	48	100	108	98	=604				

What are the values for: Σfd_y, Σfd_x^2 and $\Sigma\Sigma fm$?

* * *

$$\Sigma fd_y = 25, \quad \Sigma fd_x^2 = 604, \quad \Sigma\Sigma f = m = 426$$

---

32. Formula 14 is used to calculate the correlation coefficient using the scattergram technique.

144 Using Statistics in Teaching Physical Education

Formula 14

$$r = \frac{\frac{\Sigma\Sigma fm}{N} - (c_x \cdot c_y)}{\sigma_x \cdot \sigma_y}$$

The denominator is merely the product of the standard deviations for the two sets of data.

$\frac{\Sigma\Sigma fm}{N}$ gives us the average product moment. From this is subtracted a correction for both x and y since we are still estimating the means.

Formula 14 is used to calculate a correlation coefficient for grouped data.

The correction factors (c_x and c_y) are found by the following formulas:

Formula 15

$$c_x = \frac{\Sigma f d_x}{N}$$

Formula 16

$$c_y = \frac{\Sigma f d_y}{N}$$

Substitute the appropriate data from Plate 61 into Formulas 15 and 16 and solve the equations for c_x and c_y.

* * *

$$c_x = .84, \quad c_y = .50$$

---

33. Calculation of the standard deviation is found by solving Formulas 17 and 18.

Formula 17

$$\sigma_x = \sqrt{\frac{\Sigma f d_x^2}{N} - c_x^2} = \sqrt{\frac{604}{50} - .84^2} = \sqrt{12.08 - .71} = \sqrt{11.37} = 3.7$$

Formula 18

$$\sigma_y = \sqrt{\frac{\Sigma f d_y^2}{N} - c_y^2}$$

Find σ_y.

* * *

$\sigma_y = 2.93$

---

34. From the scattergram and Formulas 15 to 18, we now have everything we need for Formula 14.

    Formula 14

    $$r = \frac{\frac{\Sigma\Sigma fm}{N} - (c_x \cdot c_y)}{\sigma_x \cdot \sigma_y} = \frac{\frac{426}{50} - (.84 \cdot .50)}{3.37(2.93)}$$

    Solve for r.

    * * *

    $r = .82$

---

35. The goodness of a correlation coefficient depends on many factors (as described in Set 5). Regardless of whether the correlation coefficient is found using grouped or ungrouped techniques, it is interpreted identically.

    In general, the following criteria can be used to evaluate a correlation coefficient.

    $$90+ = \text{excellent}$$
    $$80+ = \text{good}$$
    $$70 = \text{low}$$
    $$60- = \text{questionable}$$

146   Using Statistics in Teaching Physical Education

What was the relationship between the badminton short and long serves based on the calculated correlation coefficient? _____.

* * *

good

---

36. We also learned in Set 5 that calculating the coefficient of determination also helps interpret a relationship between two variables.

    Remember, the coefficient of determination is found by squaring the correlation coefficient (r^2). The coefficient of determination for the badminton short and long serves would be .67 ($.82^2$).

    Can you remember how to interpret this? _____

    _____

    _____.

* * *

67% of whatever is involved in executing the
short badminton serve is also involved in
executing the long badminton serve

---

37. You should now be able to set up a scattergram properly and calculate a correlation coefficient for grouped data. These procedures would be the same even if the N were much greater.

    To review, the procedures are:
    1. Prepare a matrix approximating the number of intervals you will have (see Frame 6).
    2. Determine for each variable: range, i, and establish the intervals in the matrix.
    3. Tally the pairs of scores.
    4. Estimate the mean for both variables and isolate these intervals with lines.
    5. Find f, d, fd, fd^2 for each variable.
    6. Find the moment values for each box with tallies.
    7. Multiply the frequency of each box by its moment.

8. Add the *fm* for each row and find $\Sigma\Sigma fm$.
9. Solve Formulas 15 to 18.
10. Solve Formula 14 for *r*.

EXERCISES FOR SET 8

Here are scores on a golf putting test (X) and a golf pitch and run test (Y) for 53 high school boys. Find the relationship between the two tests by constructing a scattergram and computing the correlation coefficient. Hints: Use 5–7 for the lower X interval, 4–5 for the lower Y interval, the interval 20–22 for the estimated X mean and the interval 14–15 for the estimated Y interval.

X	Y	X	Y
42	27	13	10
38	24	11	7
40	25	20	14
39	23	12	6
36	20	7	4
35	18	8	9
29	23	10	8
28	20	14	5
26	19	16	4
26	16	15	10
26	17	15	9
28	17	14	6
23	14	15	7
33	9	16	6
26	12	21	7
27	13	16	16
20	12	29	19
21	13	30	18
22	12	29	19
20	10	32	22
20	11	34	23
21	10	33	20
22	11	35	24
17	9	37	25
26	5	36	22
11	11	34	20
		22	15

Find:
a. $\Sigma f d_x$
b. $\Sigma f d_y$
c. $\Sigma f d_x^2$
d. $\Sigma f d_y^2$
e. $\Sigma\Sigma fm$
f. r

ANSWERS FOR SET 8 EXERCISES

1. a. $\Sigma f d_x = 57$
   b. $\Sigma f d_y = -6$
   c. $\Sigma f d_x^2 = 557$
   d. $\Sigma f d_y^2 = 550$
   e. $\Sigma\Sigma fm = 437$
   f. $r = .85$

SET 9
Calculating Percentiles from Grouped Data

A percentile score is understood by most everyone. If you explained to a parent that Sam's softball test score was a percentile of 95, the parent would most likely realize that 95% of Sam's class had scores which were lower than Sam's. The percentile scale differs from other normal curve scales, however, in that it does not have units of equal intervals. That is, we cannot tell whether or not the other 95% of the class had scores 1 point below or 1,500 points below Sam's raw score.

OBJECTIVES

After completion of this set you will be able to:
1. Define the terms: percentile, quartile and decile.
2. Identify the symbols Q_1, Q_2, Q_3, D_4, f_b and f_w.
3. Determine the score which lies at a given percentile for grouped data using Formula 19.
4. Determine the percentile of a specific score in a frequency distribution using Formula 20.

---

1. In Set 3 we learned that one measure of central tendency was the median. The median was defined as the midpoint of the distribution of scores. _____ % of the scores fall above and _____ % below this midpoint.

152 Using Statistics in Teaching Physical Education

* * *

50, 50

---

2. A percentile is defined as a point in the distribution identified in terms of the percentage of scores falling below it. Thus, the middle score in a distribution is the 50th percentile because 50% of the scores in the distribution fall below that middle score.

   What proportion of scores would fall below the 25th percentile?

   _____.

* * *

25%

---

3. Thus, the 60th percentile is the score in a distribution below which 60% of the scores lies. 47% of the scores lie below the score that is at the _____ percentile.

* * *

47th

---

4. Below are 40 soccer scores tabulated with a column heading f_{cum}.

   Plate 62

i	f	f_{cum}
31–33	1	
28–30	3	
25–27	5	
22–24	7	
19–21	10	
16–18	5	14
13–15	5	9
10–12	3	4
7–9	1	1

The f_{cum} represents the cumulative frequency. That is, starting at the very bottom of the frequency, the scores are progressively added. For example, 4 is the sum of 1 and 3 for the two lowest intervals, and 9 is that sum plus 5 for the next interval up.

What is the f_{cum} for the interval 19–21? _____.

* * *

24

5. Complete the f_{cum} column for Plate 62.

* * *

i	f	f_{cum}
31–33	1	40
28–30	3	39
25–27	5	36
22–24	7	31
19–21	10	24
16–18	5	14
13–15	5	9
10–12	3	4
7–9	1	1

6. The f_{cum} for the top interval should correspond with what? _____ (symbol).

* * *

N, or the total number of scores
(which is a good double check on your figure)

7. In Plate 62, how many scores occur up to and including the interval 16–18? _____.

* * *

14

8. There are 5 scores within the interval 16–18. What is the cumulative frequency *up to* this interval? _____.

* * *

9

---

9. It is very important at this point to distinguish between the frequency within an interval and the cumulative frequency up to a given interval. What is the f_{cum} up to (below) the interval 25–27? _____.

* * *

31

---

10. What is the frequency within the interval 25–27? _____.

* * *

5

---

11. These two quantities are abbreviated f_b and f_w. If f_b represents the frequency below (or cumulative frequency up to a designated interval) then f_w represents the frequency within the interval.

In Plate 62, for the interval 22–24, what is f_b? What is f_w? _____
_____.

* * *

$f_b = 24, \quad f_w = 7$

---

12. Knowing f_b and f_w enables us to calculate percentiles from a frequency distribution. We also need to recall one principle from Set 7. The exact or real limits of the whole numbers in this problem would be:

Plate 63

i	exact value
22–24	21.5–24.4
19–21	18.5–21.4
16–18	15.5–18.4

What would be the exact or real *lower limit* of the interval 19–21?

_____.

* * *

18.5

13. 18.5 represents the lower limit of the interval of scores 19–21. This lower limit is symbolized as *ll*. The *ll* of the interval 31–33 is _____.

* * *

30.5

14. In Plate 14 the 40 soccer skill test scores are listed with the f_{cum} column completed.

Plate 64

i	f	f_{cum}
31–33	1	40
28–30	3	39
25–27	5	36
22–24	7	31
19–21	10	24
16–18	5	14
13–15	5	9
10–12	3	4
7–9	1	2

156 Using Statistics in Teaching Physical Education

Suppose we wish to give the top 20% of the students A's. We need to find out what raw score is represented by the 80th percentile. This can be done by solving Formula 19.

Formula 19

$$X_{.80} = ll + \left(\frac{.8N - f_b}{f_w}\right)i$$

What do we hope to find by using Formula 19? _____

_____.

* * *

the raw score of a specified percentile
(the 80th percentile)

---

15. The first step in solving Formula 19 is to find the interval within which the desired score lies, by multiplying the specified percentile by the number of scores (Plate 63). .80 × _____ = _____?

* * *

.80 × 40 = 32

---

16. This is the 32nd score, *not* a raw score of 32. To find which interval the 32nd score falls within, proceed up the f_{cum} column until you find a cumulative number that would include the 32nd score.

What is the interval that includes the 32nd score in Plate 64?

_____.

* * *

25–27

---

17. We now know that the 80th percentile is somewhere within the interval 25–27. We can complete Formula 19 to find the raw score.

Formula 19

$$X_{.80} = ll + \left(\frac{.8N - f_b}{f_w}\right)i$$

$$= 24.5 + \left(\frac{.8(40) - 31}{5}\right)3$$

$$= 24.5 + \left(\frac{1}{5}\right)3$$

$$= 24.5 + .6$$

$$= 25.1$$

Therefore, any one who had a raw score on the soccer test of _____ or above will receive an A.

* * *

25.1

---

18. Any desired percentile score may be found using Formula 19. The 50th percentile (the median) would be in what interval of Plate 64?

_____.

* * *

$.5 \times 40 = 20$ 19–21

---

19. How do we know that the 50th percentile is within the interval 19–21?

_____
_____.

* * *

because the 20th score from the bottom of the distribution falls within the interval 19–21.

20. Solve Formula 19 for the 50th percentile (the median).

$$X_{.50} = ll + \left(\frac{.5N - f_b}{f_w}\right) i =$$

* * *

20.3

---

21. The most commonly used percentiles are the 25th, 50th and 75th. The score at the 25th percentile is known as the 1st quartile (symbol Q_1) because one quarter of the scores lie _____ it.

* * *

below

---

22. The second quartile (Q_2) is the point below which 50% of the scores lie.

   What is another name for Q_2? _____.

* * *

the median—Mdn

---

23. The third quartile (Q_3) is equivalent to what percentile? _____. What percentage of the scores lie below it? _____.

* * *

75th, 75

---

24. The symbol for the third quartile is Q_3. The symbol for the 1st and 2nd quartiles are _____ and _____.

* * *

Q_1, Q_2

25. 25% of the scores are contained between Q_1 and Q_2. What percentage of the scores are contained between Q_2 and Q_3? _____. What percentage of scores are contained between Q_1 and Q_3? _____.

* * *

25, 50

26. 50% of the scores fall between Q_1 and Q_3. This quantity is also referred to as the interquartile range.

The interquartile range includes _____ % of the scores.

* * *

50%

27. Other commonly used percentiles are 10, 20, 30, 40 and so on. These are called deciles (symbol D). Since the word decimal means 10, the 1st decile must lie at what percentile? _____.

* * *

10th

28. Any specific decile can be indicated by a subscript. The symbol for the 6th decile is D_6. What is the symbol for the 4th decile? _____.

* * *

D_4

29. _____ % of the scores would lie below D_6.

* * *

60

160 Using Statistics in Teaching Physical Education

30. The 50th percentile, Mdn, D_5 and Q_2 all refer to the _____ score.

* * *

same or middle

31. Thus far in this set we have been concerned with finding what raw score a given percentile is. Often we wish to reverse the process, that is, we have a given raw score and we want to know what the equivalent percentile is. Assume you received a score of 17 on the soccer skill test. By knowing what percentile that score is, you will know what percentage of scores lie _____ and _____ your score.

* * *

above, below

32. When you wish to determine the percentile at which a particular raw score lies, use Formula 20.

Formula 20

$$P_x = \frac{\left(\frac{X-ll}{i}\right)f_w + f_b}{N}$$

In Formula 20 the raw score value to be converted is represented by the symbol _____.

* * *

X

33. If you receive a score of 17 on the soccer skill test, your percentile would be found by substituting in Formula 20 as follows (from Plate 63):

$$P_{17} = \frac{\left(\frac{17-15.5}{3}\right)5 + 9}{40}$$

The percentile for a raw score of 17 is _____.

Calculating Percentiles from Grouped Data 161

* * *

.29

---

34. The percentile is a theoretical point in the distribution. Your percentile of .29 means that _____ % of the scores in the class lie below your score.

* * *

29

---

35. If 29% of the scores are below your score, what percent of the scores would be above your score? _____.

* * *

71%

---

36. We are still talking in percentage terms. If we want to know how many students in our class scored below our raw score of 17, we merely multiply our percentile (.29) by the number of students in the group (40).

There are _____ students who scored lower than 17.

* * *

11.6

---

37. Obviously we cannot have 11.6 students or people. Therefore, when working with percentiles we round off to the nearest whole person. Generally most calculations are carried out to three decimal places and the final figure is rounded to the nearest person.

How many students had scores below 17 (rounded to the nearest whole person)? _____.

* * *

12

38. Since the percentile is related to a theoretical midpoint of a score, and we found in Frame 35 that 71% of the people had scores above 17, how many students had scores above 17? _____ .

* * *

28 (rounded from 28.4)

39. If we know how many students are below any given point we can also find how many are above that given point by subtracting the number below the given point from the total number of students, for example, 40 − 12 = _____ .

* * *

28

40. In Plate 65 there are 40 scores obtained on a soccer dribbling test for high school girls. Group the scores into a frequency distribution and find:

a. D_7
b. Q_2
c. a percentile for a raw score of 18
d. a raw score equal to the 30th percentile

Hint. (You will need an interval column, f column and an f_{cum} column. Use 31–33 as the top interval.)

Plate 65

7	12	14	33	18
19	20	21	22	25
26	27	29	16	19
10	13	30	23	18
20	20	21	23	24
11	28	15	16	19
20	13	15	17	25
27	21	22	17	24

Calculating Percentiles from Grouped Data

* * *

i	f	f_{cum}
31–33	1	40
28–30	3	39
25–27	5	36
22–24	6	31
19–21	10	25
16–18	6	15
13–15	5	9
10–12	3	4
7–9	1	1

a. $X_p = ll + \left(\dfrac{?N - f_b}{f_w} \right) i = X_{.70} = 21.5 + \left(\dfrac{28 - 25}{6} \right) 3 \qquad X_{.70} = 23$ or $D_7 = 23$

b. $X_p = ll + \left(\dfrac{?N - f_b}{f_w} \right) i = X_{.50} = 18.5 + \left(\dfrac{20 - 15}{10} \right) 3 \qquad X_{.50} = 20$ or $Q_2 = 20$

c. $P_x = \dfrac{\left(\dfrac{X - ll}{i} \right) f_w + f_b}{N} = P_{18} = \dfrac{\left(\dfrac{18 - 15.5}{3} \right) 6 + 9}{40} \qquad P_{18} = .35$

d. $X_p = ll + \left(\dfrac{?N - f_b}{f_w} \right) i = X_{.30} = 15.5 + \left(\dfrac{12 - 9}{6} \right) 3 \qquad X_{.30} = 17$

---

41. Percentiles are useful to determine the percentage of cases or students within a given set of boundaries, that is, below a certain point on a scale (Q_3) or between D_2 and D_3. However, percentiles are limited somewhat in their use in that there is no way to know how the scores between Q_1 and Q_2 are distributed. We only know that _____ % of the scores lie somewhere within these limits.

* * *

25

EXERCISES FOR SET 9

1. Define the following terms:

   a. percentile

   b. quartile

   c. decile

2. Identify the following symbols by matching Column A and Column B.

Column A	Column B
____ a. 25th percentile	f_w
____ b. cumulative frequency up to (or below)	f_b
____ c. 75th percentile	D_4
____ d. 4th decile	Q_3
____ e. frequency within an interval	Q_2
____ f. Mdn	Q_1

3. From the following distribution, complete the f_{cum} column and calculate:

   a. D_4 ⎫
   b. Q_3 ⎬ Formula 19

   c. percentile for a raw score of 22 ⎫
   d. how many people received a raw score below 29 ⎬ Formula 20

   The following distribution represents 100 scores received by high school girls on a motor ability test. The scores represent time in seconds.

i	f	f_{cum}
37–38	2	
35–36	3	
33–34	4	
31–32	7	
29–30	11	
27–28	16	
25–26	19	
23–24	12	
21–22	9	
19–20	9	
17–18	3	
15–16	4	
13–14	1	

Formula 19

$$X_p = ll + \left(\frac{?N - f_b}{f_w}\right)i$$

Formula 20

$$P_x = \frac{\left(\dfrac{X - ll}{i}\right)f_w + f_b}{N}$$

ANSWERS FOR SET 9 EXERCISES

1. a. Percentile—A point in a distribution of scores in terms of the percentage of scores falling below it.
   b. Quartile—When a distribution is divided into four parts, each quarter or 25% is called a quartile. Q_1, Q_2, Q_3 represent the 25th, 50th and 75th percentiles.
   c. Decile—When a distribution of scores is divided into 10 parts, each 1/10 or 10% is called a decile. D_3, D_6, D_9 represent the 30th, 60th and 90th percentiles.

2. a. Q_1 d. D_4
   b. f_b e. f_w
   c. Q_3 f. Q_2

3.

i	f	f_{cum}
37–38	2	100
35–36	3	98
33–34	4	95
31–32	7	91
29–30	11	84
27–28	16	73
25–26	19	57
23–24	12	38
21–22	9	26
19–20	9	17
17–18	3	8
15–16	4	5
13–14	1	1

a. $X_{p=40} = 24.71$ sec.
b. $X_{p=75} = 28.86$ sec.
c. $P_{x=22} = .24$
d. $P_{x=29} = .76$ or 76 people ($.76 \times 100$)

SET 10

Grading Systems

Grading systems used in physical education programs range from the most simple "subjective mark" through the more complex systems involving the use of descriptive statistics. This set does not aim to examine the relative merits of grading systems such as the "parent conference"; pass-fail; A, S, F; and letter or number grades. Rather, this set teaches how to compute physical education grades by some common methods using elementary statistical procedures.

OBJECTIVES

At the conclusion of this set you will be able to:

1. Explain the relationship between weighting of marks and philosophy of evaluation.
2. Assign final grades to a group of students using the simplified letter grade system.
3. Assign final grades to a group of students using the scale score method.
4. Assign final grades to a group of students using the "total points" method.

---

1. Each portion of a final grade will be given a certain emphasis depending on the teacher's philosophy. The emphasis given to a

specific portion of a grade is called the weight. For example, if teacher A believes that skill should determine 90% of a student's grade, and teacher B believes that skill should determine 45% of a student's grade, the two teachers differ in their philosophy of grading.

How would they probably reflect that difference on the final grade?

_____

_____.

* * *

by giving different weight (emphasis) to the final mark for skill

2. It could be said that in Frame 1, teacher A believed skill was twice as important a part of the grade as did teacher B. If teacher A believed that knowledge should determine 40% of the final grade and teacher B does not believe a grade in physical education should include knowledge, the different weight given to knowledge would reflect what difference between teachers A and B? _____

_____.

* * *

the difference in their philosophy of grading

3. The weight of a particular portion of the final grade, then depends on its relative importance in a particular teacher's philosophy. If teacher A decides he will make skill 60% of the final grade and knowledge 20% of the final grade he is saying, in effect, that he thinks skill is how many times as important as knowledge? _____.

* * *

3 times

4. Assume a teacher wishes to include in the final grade the following: skill, physical fitness, knowledge and attitude. There are four components in the total grade. If each component were equally weighted, what percent of the grade would each factor contribute? _____.

* * *

25%

---

5. If an unequal weighting system were used, one could assign skill 50%, physical fitness 20% and knowledge 20%. How much of the final grade would be left for attitude? _____.

* * *

10%

---

6. Weights for portions of a grade merely adjust actual values to a predetermined proportion. These proportions can be any combination of numbers based on your belief of what the final grade should be. In order to inject our philosophy of what physical education evaluation should be, we weight specific portions of the final grade.

The weighting for the previous example would be skill 5, physical fitness 2, knowledge 2 and attitude 1. Remember, however, that these weights are arbitrary.

Could the weights have been 5, 4, 4, 3? _____.

* * *

yes

---

7. Now let's look at the first grading system. Letter grades A, B, C, etc., can be transformed to numbers 1, 2, 3, etc. The letter grade A could be equivalent to a 5, letter grade B to 4, etc., or the letter grade A

172   Using Statistics in Teaching Physical Education

could be equivalent to a 1, B to 2, etc. If letter grade A equals 5, to what would a letter grade of C be transformed? _____.

* * *

3

---

8. Transformations of letter grades to number grades are shown in Plate 66.

   Plate 66

Letter grade	A	B	C	D	F
Transformation 1	5	4	3	2	1
Transformation 2	1	2	3	4	5

   Using transformation 1, the number 2 represents which letter grade?

   _____ .

* * *

D

---

9. We now have the necessary tools to demonstrate the first grading system. We first list the factors to be included in the final grade. Next add weights.

   Plate 67

Factor	Weight
Skill	3
Fitness	2
Knowledge	2
Improvement	1
Attitude	1

   The philosophy prevalent in this weighting indicates that skill is how many times as important as improvement? _____. And fitness is how many times more important than attitude?_____.

* * *

3, 2

---

10. We add to Plate 67 actual grades received by a student (letter grades transformed to numbers, A = 5, B = 4, etc.). We next multiply the weight times the grade to get the number of adjusted points for each portion of the grade.

Plate 68

Factor	Weight	Grade	Points
Skill (3)			
test 1	1	C (3)	3
test 2	1	A (5)	5
test 3	1	C (3)	3
Fitness	2	B (4)	8
Knowledge	2	C (3)	6
Improvement	1	B (4)	4
Attitude	1	A (5)	5
Total =			

Find the total weights and total number of points.

* * *

9, 34

---

11. The final grade is found by dividing the total weighted points by the total number of weights. What would the final numerical grade be for the student in Plate 68? _____.

* * *

3.78

12. What would the number 3.78 convert to in a letter system?

    Plate 69

    $$A = 5$$
    $$B = 4$$
    $$C = 3 \quad \leftarrow 3.78$$
    $$D = 2$$
    $$F = 1$$

    * * *

    B —

13. This system of grading is particularly useful when the teacher likes to use the letter grade with every individual mark. An additional advantage is that students are familiar with what letter grades mean. If this type of grading system was used and the following weighted factors were selected, what would be the final numerical and letter grade for a student who received the noted letter marks? _____.

    Plate 70

Factor	Weight	Grade	Points
Skill	2	A	
Knowledge	1	B	
Improvement	3	C	

    * * *

    3.83, B

14. The second system we will consider uses a point system. Simply stated, with this system we merely assign a certain number of points to each factor of the grade. A final grade, then, would be determined by a total number of points accumulated by adding points for each factor.

Grading Systems 175

We learned in Set 6, however, that whenever we add different kinds of quantities we have to convert those different kinds of quantities into a common scale. If we want to add two unlike quantities, such as tumbling scores and "time to run the mile", we must first convert the scores to what? _____ _____ .

* * *

scale scores

---

15. Herein lies the value of scale scoring for grading systems.

    Each time a test is given or a measurement made, the raw scores obtained are converted to scale scores. Weights are assigned in the same manner as in the letter grade system. The initial step in the numerical system of grading is to convert the raw scores to scale scores of some type. If we want to eliminate negative signs, we can use any of which three scales? _____ .

* * *

T, Hull or sigma scales

---

16. As with the letter system, we need to weight the portions of the final grade as we feel they are important.

    Assume we wish to grade one particular class as follows: Skill and fitness 40%, Social 40% and Knowledge 20%. What are the respective weights? _____ .

* * *

4, 4, 2

---

17. Reducing the weights, if possible, keeps numbers lower when multiplying. What would the weighting be for Frame 16 if they were reduced? _____ .

* * *

2, 2, 1

---

18. Let's examine the 40% skill and fitness for a moment. This may be only one score, or it may be the average of 3 or 4 subtests. Whether 40% skill and fitness represents one test or the average of 4 tests, it still is weighted _____ in the example shown in Frames 16 and 17.

* * *

2

---

19. Plate 71 shows how this system could be entered in a record book.

    Plate 71

	Skill & Fitness 40%		Social 40%		Knowledge 20%		Total
	Raw Score	Scale Score	Raw Score	Scale Score	Raw Score	Scale Score	
Weight	65	55 2 --- 110	40	20 2 --- 40	65	28 1 --- 28	178

Remember, each scale score has a mean of 50. If that measure has a weight of 2, the weighted scale score mean would be 100.

Hint. Use red pen for scale scores. What would be the mean of the weighted scale score for skill and fitness?

* * *

100

20. How many weights make up a total weighted scale score in Plate 71?

* * *

5

---

21. If we multiply the total number of weights by the mean scale score of 50, we know that the total weighted scale mean will be _____.

* * *

250

---

22. We can now observe the relationship of the sample grade with the class mean. The sample student in Plate 71 was 72 weighted scale score points below the mean. We can also analyze each of his marks independently since we know the mean of each scale is 50.

The sample student in Plate 71 was above the mean on which one mark? _____.

* * *

skill and fitness

---

23. The end product of this system is a total point value. Some way must be devised to convert or transform this total number of points to a final letter grade.

One method often used to transform scores to letter grades is to apply the normal probability curve. This term, however, is often misunderstood. There are many different ways to grade "according to the normal curve."

Remember, the assumption underlying the normal probability curve is that the scores are normally distributed and the two halves of the curve are _____.

178 Using Statistics in Teaching Physical Education

* * *

symmetrical or the same

---

24. You may remember from Set 6 that the normal curve, when divided into 6 parts (±3 σ), includes 99.73 percent of all cases (for practical purposes, 100% of our group), and from a table we can find the proportion of people in any area under this curve. For grading purposes, the normal curve with its 6 standard units (100%) can be divided into any desired number of parts.

Plate 72

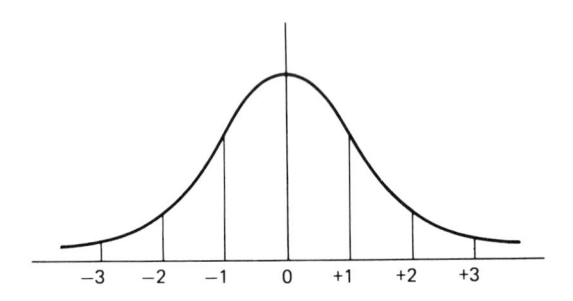

How many standard deviation units make up the normal curve?

_____.

* * *

6

---

25. To grade by the normal curve, using any system, one need merely divide 6 by the number of categories desired. If we wanted to grade with the normal curve and believed in giving A, B, C and D grades, we would first divide 6 by 4 in order to determine the standard deviation unit. $4\overline{)6.0}$ = ? _____.

Grading Systems 179

* * *

1.5

---

26. Plate 73 illustrates the normal curve divided into four parts.

    Plate 73

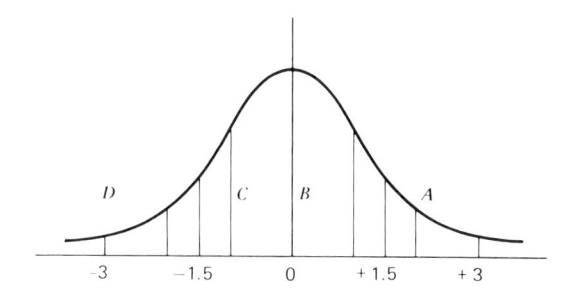

```
              |
           ___|___
          /   |   \
        /  C  | B   \
      / D    |      A \
    /_____|_____
   -3    -1.5    0   +1.5   +3
```

By referring to Table 1 in Set 6 (page 88) we can find the exact percentage of pupils falling under the normal curve between 0 and 1.5 σ and between 1.5 and 3.0 σ. What percent of the students, using this system, would receive A's, B's, C's and D's? _____

_____.

* * *

A = 6.55%   B = 43.32%   C = 43.32%   D = 6.55%

---

27. This procedure can be duplicated with various other systems, for example, ABC; ABCDF. When dividing the six normal units by an odd number of categories, that is, 3 or 5, one unit will have to straddle the midline of the curve. $3\overline{)6.0}$ = ? _____.

180 Using Statistics in Teaching Physical Education

* * *

2.0

---

28. Each of the three final categories, that is, A B C, will consist of 2 standard deviations. The middle category will have to straddle the mean of the normal curve.

    Plate 74

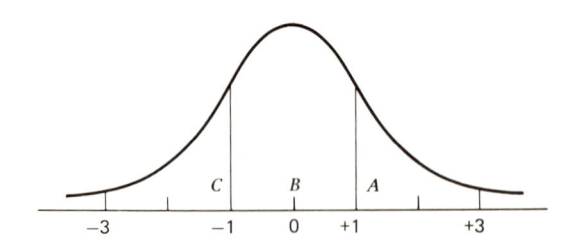

    C   B   A
    −3   −1   0   +1   +3

    What percent of the cases will get A's, B's and C's? _____

    _____ .

    * * *

    A = 15.74%   B = 68.26%   C = 15.74%

---

29. In order to examine what happens to numerical scores using various techniques Plate 75 lists total weighted points for a class of high school girls ($N = 32$). We shall use 5 different techniques to assign letter grades as follows:

    1. Pass-Fail
    2. A B C ─┐
    3. A B C D ├─ using the normal curve
    4. A B C D F ─┘
    5. Cluster system

Plate 75

1. Pass-Fail
2. A B C
3. A B C D
4. A B C D F
5. Cluster system

Total Points	1	2	3	4	5
649					
632					
619					
598					
548					
525					
520					
516					
516					
510					
440					
350					
345					
345					
320					
318					
310					
305					
298					
282					
280					
275					
260					
250					
245					
240					
230					
200					
190					
140					
135					
98					

Total points are listed in what order? _____.

* * *

descending

---

30. Even though technique 1 is merely pass-fail, a decision must be made as to where the cut-off point will be. A line may be drawn at a set percent, the scores may be inspected for a break in the distribution, or a combination of both. If we said the bottom 10% would fail, how many students would this be? (Plate 75, $N=32$). _____.

* * *

three

---

31. Let's inspect the distribution of scores for breaks or gaps where there is a great distance between points. Between the 1st and 2nd score there is a difference of 17 points (649–632); between the 2nd and 3rd scores, 13 points; between the 3rd and 4th scores, 21 points; between the 4th and 5th scores, 50 points; and between the 5th and 6th scores, 23 points.

    If you wanted to give 4 or 5 A's, would the gap in the distribution of scores favor giving 4 A's or 5? _____.

* * *

4

---

32. If we had decided that the lower 30% would fail, which score would be the lowest to pass? _____.

* * *

275

33. Many factors enter into the decision as to where one would draw the line on a pass-fail mark. There is always a decision to be made. For our purposes, draw a horizontal line in column 1 between the scores 260 and 275.

How many students would fail? _____.

* * *

10

---

34. In column 2 we will show the method using the normal curve when we believe in giving only A's, B's and C's in physical education. In Frame 27 we found that by dividing 6 by 3 we have 2 standard deviations in each category. There will be 15.87% A's and C's and 68.23% B's. Multiply each of these percentages by N and draw the lines in the appropriate places in column 2. What scores will receive A's. _____.

* * *

548 and above

---

35. What scores will receive C's in column 2? _____.

* * *

200 and below

---

36. In column 3 we have a four letter system based on the normal curve, that is, A, B, C, D. Dividing 6 by 4 gives us 1.5 standard deviations for each category. Table 1 tells us that 6.68% will receive A's and D's, and 43.32% will receive B's and C's. How many students will receive each of the 4 grades? _____.

184 Using Statistics in Teaching Physical Education

* * *

A=2, B=14, C=14, D=2

---

37. Draw horizontal lines between the four categories in column 3, of Plate 75. What is the top score in the B bracket? _____.

* * *

619

---

38. In column 4 we will use the traditional 5 letter system using the normal curve, that is, A B C D F. Dividing 6 by 5 gives us 1.2 standard deviation units for each grade category. Since we have an odd number of categories, which category will have to straddle the mean? _____.

* * *

middle, or C

---

39. Since the C category will straddle the mean, one-half the standard deviation unit (1.2) will be on one side of the mean and one-half will be on the other side of the mean. This value is _____.

* * *

.6

---

40. Plate 76 shows how the normal curve is divided into 5 parts with the middle category straddling the mean.

Grading Systems 185

Plate 76

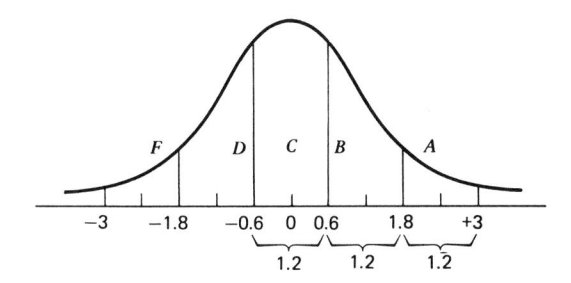

```
           F   D   C   B   A
        -3  -1.8  -0.6 0 0.6  1.8  +3
                  \__/\__/\__/
                  1.2  1.2  1.2
```

What percentage of students would receive A's, B's and C's? _____

* * *

A = 3.46%   B = 23.84%   C = 45.14%

---

41. How many students will get A's, B's, C's, D's and F's under this system? (Round off to the nearest person.) _____.

* * *

A = 1   B = 8   C = 14   D = 8   F = 1

---

42. What was the lowest C grade in Column 4? _____.

* * *

260

---

43. When using the normal curve in grading, what do we know about the number of grades on either side of the midpoint? _____.

186 Using Statistics in Teaching Physical Education

* * *

the same number of grades appears on each side
of the midpoint

---

44. In the last column (5) we will use the cluster system. With the cluster system the teacher scans the distribution of scores watching for large gaps in the numbers rather than following the normal curve exactly. Here, too, the teacher expresses a grading philosophy in deciding how many and what kind of grades to give. Since all measurement is imperfect, it would be unwise to make a demarcation where there was a small gap or no gap in the descending numbers. If a decision must be made for a change in grade where there is little or no gap in the numbers, the teacher should then look at names of students receiving those close scores and make a professional judgment as to which student is most or least deserving of the "benefit of the doubt." Assume here that we want to give 5 letter grades, A, B, C, D, F, but we do not want to follow the normal curve. Scanning down the numbers in Plate 75 we find a gap of 50 points between 598 and 548. Continue in this manner until you have made demarcations for each of the 5 letter grades. When completed, compare your Plate 75 with Plate 77.

* * *

---

45. Plate 77 shows how grades for a class would be given using five different systems.

What would the student receiving a total point score of 245 get for a grade under the five systems? 1 =   , 2 =   , 3 =   , 4 =   , 5 =   .

* * *

1 = F, 2 = B, 3 = C, 4 = D, 5 = D

Plate 77

Total points	1	2	3	4	5
649			A	A	
632		A			
619					A
598					
548				B	
525	P				
520			B		B
516					
516					
510					
440					
350					
345				C	
345					
320		B			C
318					
310					
305					
298					
282					
280					
275			C		
260					
250					
245					
240	F				D
230					
200				D	
190					
140		C			
135			D		F
98				F	

EXERCISES FOR SET 10

1. Explain briefly the relationship of grading to a philosophy of physical education.

2. Assume a student is enrolled in a physical education course where the simplified letter grade system of grading is used (A=5, B=4, C=3, D=2, F=1) and the following content existed:

Factor	Weight	Grade
Skill	3	A
Knowledge	2	D
Sportsmanship	1	C
Attitude	1	C
Fitness	1	C

   What would be his final point and letter grade?

3. Assume a senior student in a golf class received the following:

Factor	Hull Scale Scores	Weight
Skill	62	3
Knowledge	57	2
Attendance	68	1

   How many total weighted points would he have? Would he be above or below the class weighted mean?

4. In the table are scores that represent total weighted points for a semester physical education course. Determine grades for the 42 students using the following five systems:
   1. pass-fail
   2. ABC
   3. ABCD ⎫ using the normal curve
   4. ABCDF ⎭
   5. the cluster system

Total Points	1	2	3	4	5
706					
653					
641					
622					
622					
621					
610					
610					
585					
577					
576					
576					
574					
551					
550					
543					
520					
515					
489					
486					
480					
475					
461					
454					
429					
425					
423					
419					
418					
418					
404					
401					
392					
369					
360					
344					
340					
325					
318					
313					
311					
309					

ANSWERS FOR SET 10 EXERCISES

1. A philosophy of physical education will dictate which system of grading will be used and how much emphasis will be placed on each phase of the grade.
2. 3.5 C+ or B-
3. 368 points, above the mean
4. See table on opposite page

4.

Total points	1	2	3	4	5
706				A	
653			A		
641		A			A
622					
622				B	
621					
610					
610					
585			B		
577	P				B
576					
576					
574					
551					
550		B			
543					
520					
515					
489				C	
486					
480					C
475					
461					
454					
429					
425			C		
423					
419					
418					
418					
404					
401					
392					
369					D
360					
344				D	
340					
325					
318	F	C			F
313					
311			D		
309				F	

SET 11

Comparing Group Performance

Thus far, we have been discussing statistical techniques applied to physical education that describe a state, that is, average, variability, relationships, and so on. Often we want to find out if two groups of students differ significantly on a particular test. In other words, we want to know if one group is superior on some particular trait, for example, strength, fitness or skill.

There are several different formulas used for this purpose. Basically the one used depends on whether there is an equal number of students in the group and whether the data consist of two sets of measurements on the same group or on different groups. If you are interested in comparing more than two groups, see your instructor for assistance. Those data require the use of analysis of variance, which is beyond the scope of this book.

OBJECTIVES

After completion of this set you should be able to determine whether two means are significantly different when:

1. The groups being compared are different people, and
2. A group is being measured a second time.

---

1. We will consider first how to compare two different groups of students.

Let us assume for a sample problem that we have tested two eighth grade classes on a field hockey shooting accuracy test. We want to find out which class is, on the average, the better of the two. For practical purposes we will use numbers smaller than an actual class of students in order to keep computation to a minimum. Let us assume for a moment that the means for the two groups are 36 and 38. It is obvious that 38 is larger than 36. To determine whether this mean difference is real, or merely due to chance, what else would you suggest we look at? _____

_____.

* * *

the variability of the scores
(also, as we shall see later, the size of the group)

---

2. In addition to looking at the means and variability of the scores, we would also need to know the number of students in each group. If we had 200 students in each group, the 38 might reflect very different raw scores than the 36. If we had only 15 in the group, the mean difference of 2 could merely be due to a small group sample variation.

   In addition to $\overline{X}$ and σ, we should examine what other characteristic of the data? _____.

* * *

n, or N, or the number of students in each group

---

3. Gossett, in 1931, developed a t statistic to test whether two means are really different or are merely due to chance.

   The t test, then, is used to compare what? _____.

* * *

group means

---

4. The formula for finding t is shown below. The formula looks complicated but is really quite simple.

Formula 21

$$t = \frac{\bar{X}_1 - \bar{X}_2}{\sqrt{\left[\dfrac{\Sigma X_1^2 - \dfrac{(\Sigma X_1)^2}{n_1} + \Sigma X_2^2 - \dfrac{(\Sigma X_2)^2}{n_2}}{(n_1 + n_2) - 2}\right]\left[\dfrac{1}{n_1} + \dfrac{1}{n_2}\right]}}$$

Examine Formula 21 carefully. Does it contain any symbols that have not previously been used in this book? _____.

* * *

no

---

5. No! There are no new symbols at all. You already know how to find everything required in the formula. List the symbols you need to solve equation 21. _____
   _____.

* * *

$\Sigma X_1 \quad \Sigma X_2 \quad \Sigma X_1^2 \quad \Sigma X_2^2 \quad n_1 \quad n_2 \quad \bar{X}_1 \quad \bar{X}_2$

---

6. Now we will return to the original problem of comparing two classes on the field hockey shooting accuracy test.

   In Plate 78 the original raw scores for the two groups are found.

   Plate 78

X_1	X_1^2	X_2	X_2^2
4		2	
4		3	
6		3	
4		3	
7		3	
5		4	
3			
6			
4			
7			

Using Statistics in Teaching Physical Education

Find:

$\Sigma X_1 =$ $n_1 =$

$\Sigma X_2 =$ $n_2 =$

$\Sigma X_1^2 =$ $\overline{X}_1 =$

$\Sigma X_2^2 =$ $\overline{X}_2 =$

* * *

$\Sigma X_1 = 50$ $n_1 = 10$
$\Sigma X_2 = 18$ $n_2 = 6$
$\Sigma X_1^2 = 268$ $\overline{X}_1 = 5$
$\Sigma X_2^2 = 56$ $\overline{X}_2 = 3$

---

7. Now you have all the information you need for finding t. Plug the information into Formula 21, and solve for t.

$$t = \frac{\overline{X}_1 - \overline{X}_2}{\sqrt{\left[\frac{\Sigma X_1^2 - \frac{(\Sigma X_1)^2}{n_1} + \Sigma X_2^2 - \frac{(\Sigma X_2)^2}{n_2}}{(n_1 + n_2) - 2}\right]\left[\frac{1}{n_1} + \frac{1}{n_2}\right]}}$$

$$t = \frac{5-3}{\sqrt{\left[\dfrac{268 - \dfrac{(50)^2}{10} + 56 - \dfrac{(18)^2}{6}}{10+6-2}\right]\left[\dfrac{1}{10} + \dfrac{1}{6}\right]}}$$

$t = 3.22$

---

8. We now have solved the equation and found that the value for t is 3.22.

   What is this test called? _____.

   * * *

   t test

---

9. This figure, by itself, means nothing. Statisticians have developed tables, however, which help us to assess the meaning of our t value. These tables tell us whether our mean differences are significant or whether the differences are probably due to randomly occurring events.

   Two means are hardly ever exactly the same. What does the t test tell us? _____

   _____.

   * * *

   whether the difference is real or
   significant, or merely due to chance

---

10. Before we compare our t of 3.22 with a table value we need to learn three more bits of information. The first is a term called "degree of freedom." The theory behind this term is beyond the scope of this

program, however. For this type of group comparison the "degrees of freedom" (symbol *df*) is simply $n_1 + n_2 - 1$.

If group 1 had 36 subjects and group 2 had 38 subjects, how many degrees of freedom would the problem have? _____.

* * *

df = 73
($n_1 + n_2 - 1$ or $36 + 38 - 1$)

---

11. Remember, a small *n* indicates the number of students in one group. What are the degrees of freedom for the problem in Plate 78? _____.

* * *

15

---

12. To analyze the *t* value we must also establish the degree of accuracy we desire. The term used for this purpose is called the probability level.

Suppose your school was going on a field trip. Twenty buses were going but it was known that one bus would be involved in a fatal crash. Would you go on the field trip? Most likely not, since the probability of your getting killed that day would be one in twenty, or to say it another way, 5 students out of every 100 would die; or yet another way, 5% (.05) would die. When life is at stake those odds are not too good. In comparing mean performance of groups of students, however, we can accept those odds. That is to say, assuming all other things to be constant, we would expect that if we tested 100 groups of 10th grade students on a performance test, the group means would be approximately the same 95 times out of 100. How many times would we expect—under normal conditions—that the means would not be approximately the same? _____.

* * *

5 times, .05 or 5%

Comparing Group Performance   199

13. The probability level is arbitrarily selected by the investigator. In physical education the probability level is usually .05 or .01. In medical research it may be .001, and in social science work it may be .10.

   The probability level indicates what about the statistic t? _____

   * * *

   accuracy demanded

---

14. Most of the time when we compare groups, we assume for test purposes that the means will be nearly the same. This is referred to as "accepting the null hypothesis" (symbol H_0).

   If we assume the means to be approximately the same, we say we are testing the _____ hypothesis.

   * * *

   null or H_0

---

15. In physical education we generally test the null hypothesis at the .05 probability level (occasionally at the .01 level). The t table (Table 2) shows the probability level desired across the top and the degrees of freedom down the left hand margin.

   The most frequently used level of accuracy in physical education when comparing group means is the _____ probability level.

   * * *

   .05

---

16. If we look at Table 2 for the .05 probability level for 90 df we find a value of 1.99. In order for the two groups to be considered significantly different, the t value obtained from Formula 21 must exceed

the value in Table 2. If your calculated t is less than the tabled value the groups are really at about the same skill level.

What is the tabled value for a probability of .05 with 15 df? _____.

* * *

2.13

TABLE 2. Table of Critical Values of t

df	.05	.01
1	12.706	63.657
2	4.303	9.925
3	3.182	5.841
4	2.776	4.604
5	2.571	4.032
6	2.447	3.707
7	2.365	3.499
8	2.306	3.355
9	2.262	3.250
10	2.228	3.169
11	2.201	3.106
12	2.179	3.055
13	2.160	3.012
14	2.145	2.977
15	2.131	2.947
16	2.120	2.921
17	2.110	2.898
18	2.101	2.878
19	2.093	2.861
20	2.086	2.845
21	2.080	2.831
22	2.074	2.819
23	2.069	2.807
24	2.064	2.797
25	2.060	2.787

Continued

Comparing Group Performance 201

TABLE 2. (*Continued*)

df	.05	.01
26	2.056	2.779
27	2.052	2.771
28	2.048	2.763
29	2.045	2.756
30	2.042	2.750
40	2.021	2.704
60	2.000	2.660
120	1.980	2.617
∞	1.960	2.576

17. Now compare the table value of 2.13 with your calculated *t* in Frame 7.

    Is your calculated value higher or lower than the table *t* value for the .05 probability level and 15 *df*? _____.

    * * *

    higher

18. Since your calculated *t* value is higher, would you accept or reject the null hypothesis (that is, that there is no significant difference between the means)? _____.

    * * *

    reject

19. If we reject the idea that there is no difference between the means, we are really saying that there *is* a difference between the two means.

    Therefore, we conclude that group one was better skilled on the field hockey shooting accuracy test than group 2.

    * * *

20. Here is a summary of the procedures to determine if two means differ significantly.
    1. Find:

       $\Sigma X_1 =$ $n_1 =$

       $\Sigma X_2 =$ $n_2 =$

       $\Sigma X_1^2 =$ $\bar{X}_1 =$

       $\Sigma X_2^2 =$ $\bar{X}_2 =$

    2. Find t using Formula 21.
    3. Determine the degrees of freedom. $df = N - 1$
    4. Select the desired probability level (usually .05).
    5. State the problem using the null hypothesis (H_0).
    6. Find the tabled value for t.
    7. Compare your calculated t with the tabled value.
    8. Accept or reject the null hypothesis and formulate your conclusion.

    * * *

21. Two women teachers in junior high wish to compare how much their respective classes have learned about the rules in the game of field hockey. They develop a written test and give it to their classes. The scores were:

    Plate 79

Teacher A		Teacher B	
X_1	X_1^2	X_2	X_2^2
15		8	
8		9	
3		7	
14		4	
7		3	
13		5	
12		6	
9		8	
11		7	
13		4	
14			
10			

Find: a.

$$\Sigma X_1 = \qquad n_1 =$$
$$\Sigma X_2 = \qquad n_2 =$$
$$\Sigma X_1^2 = \qquad \overline{X}_1 =$$
$$\Sigma X_2^2 = \qquad \overline{X}_2 =$$

b. $t =$
c. $df =$
d. was one group better than the other? (Use a probability level of .05)

$$t = \frac{\overline{X}_1 - \overline{X}_2}{\sqrt{\left[\frac{\Sigma X_1^2 - \frac{(\Sigma X_1)^2}{n_1} + \Sigma X_2^2 - \frac{(\Sigma X_2)^2}{n_2}}{(n_1 + n_2) - 2}\right]\left[\frac{1}{n_1} + \frac{1}{n_2}\right]}}$$

$df = N - 1$

* * *

a.

$$\Sigma X_1 = 129 \qquad n_1 = 12$$
$$\Sigma X_2 = 61 \qquad n_2 = 10$$
$$\Sigma X_1^2 = 1523 \qquad \overline{X}_1 = 10.75$$
$$\Sigma X_2^2 = 409 \qquad \overline{X}_2 = 6.1$$

b. $t = 3.69$
c. $df = 21$
d. yes

$$t = \frac{10.75 - 6.1}{\sqrt{\left[\frac{1523 - \frac{(129)^2}{12} + 409 - \frac{(61)^2}{10}}{(12 + 10) - 2}\right]\left[\frac{1}{12} + \frac{1}{10}\right]}}$$

22. Now we will consider how to compare group means when the same group is tested twice. Assume we are teaching a class in tennis. We administer a tennis skills test to our class at the beginning of the term (or after a few weeks of instruction), and again at the end of the course. We want to see, by comparing the two means, if there has been a significant improvement.

If we found the first test mean to be 64 and the second test mean to be 66, would it necessarily mean that there had been improvement?___

* * *

no

23. The primary difference between this procedure and comparing different group means is that we have exactly the same number of students in each group. That is, each student is pretested and posttested. Therefore we will be working with a pair of scores for each student. N will represent the total number of pairs of scores. If a student was absent during either the pre- or post test, his score could not be used in the analysis.

In comparing means using the same group measured twice, what does N represent? _____.

* * *

the number of pairs of scores

24. We still use the t test here, but apply a different formula. Formula 22 is used for finding the significance of the difference between means obtained for the same group.

Formula 22

$$t = \frac{\bar{X}_1 - \bar{X}_2}{\sqrt{\dfrac{\Sigma D^2 - \dfrac{(\Sigma D)^2}{N}}{N(N-1)}}}$$

Comparing Group Performance   205

D represents the difference between each pair of scores.

How would you verbalize the expression $\dfrac{(\Sigma D)^2}{N}$? _____

_____

_____.

* * *

$\dfrac{(\Sigma D)^2}{N}$ = the sum of the differences of pairs of scores, quantity squared, then divided by the number of pairs of scores

25. Looking at Formula 22, list the symbols you need for solving for t and verbalize what the symbols mean. (e.g., $\overline{X}_1$ = the mean for the first test.)

$$t = \dfrac{\overline{X}_1 - \overline{X}_2}{\sqrt{\dfrac{\Sigma D^2 - \dfrac{(\Sigma D)^2}{N}}{N(N-1)}}}$$

* * *

$\overline{X}_1$ the mean for the first test
$\overline{X}_2$ the mean for the second test
D the difference between each pair of scores
ΣD the sum of the differences for each pair of scores
ΣD^2 the difference between each score—squared—then the squares are added
N the number of pairs of scores

26. For computational purposes, only the absolute difference between the means in the formula is necessary. Since we are comparing a class mean after instruction with a class mean before instruction, which mean would you expect to be greater? _____

_____.

206 Using Statistics in Teaching Physical Education

* * *

the second test mean (therefore we would disregard the minus sign for the mean difference. It must be remembered, however, for the final analysis, which mean was greater.)

---

27. In Plate 80, the scores for the first and second tests are presented and the D and D^2 columns are partially completed.

Plate 80

first test	second test	D	D^2
23	28	+5	25
32	31	−1	1
25	31	+6	36
25	32	+7	49
20	28	+8	
16	26		
21	30		
23	21		
22	28		
26	34		
		$\Sigma D =$	$\Sigma D^2 =$

Find: ΣD
ΣD^2
$\overline{X}_1$
$\overline{X}_2$
N

* * *

$\Sigma D = 56$

$\Sigma D^2 = 460$

$\overline{X}_1 = 23.3$

$\overline{X}_2 = 28.9$

$N = 10$

28. You now have all the information you need for finding t. Plug the information into Formula 22 and solve for t.

$$t = \frac{\overline{X}_1 - \overline{X}_2}{\sqrt{\dfrac{\Sigma D^2 - \dfrac{(\Sigma D)^2}{N}}{N(N-1)}}}$$

$$t =$$

* * *

$$t = \frac{23.3 - 28.9}{\sqrt{\dfrac{460 - \dfrac{(56)^2}{10}}{10(10-1)}}}$$

$$t = 4.38$$

29. The degrees of freedom for comparing means of the *same group* are calculated differently than df for comparing different group means.

Here we are working with pairs of scores, therefore $df = N - 1$. Remember, N represents the number of pairs of scores.

What are the degrees of freedom for the problem in Plate 80 in Frame 27? _____.

* * *

9, $df = N - 1$, or $10 - 1$

30. The remainder of the analysis is identical to comparing different groups' means. Here is a summary of the procedures to determine if two means, taken from the same group of students, differ significantly:

1. Find $\Sigma D =$ $\overline{X}_1 =$ $N =$
   $\Sigma D^2 =$ $\overline{X}_2 =$
2. Find t using Formula 22.
3. Determine the degrees of freedom $df = N - 1$ (N is the number of pairs of scores).
4. Select the desired probability level (usually .05).
5. State the problem using the null hypothesis (H_0).
6. Find the tabled value for t.
7. Compare your calculated t with the tabled value.
8. Accept or reject the null hypothesis and formulate your conclusion.

In Frame 28 the calculated t was 4.38. The $df = N - 1$, or 9. Selecting the probability level of .01, is the calculated t value greater than or less than the tabled value _____. Would we reject the null hypothesis or accept it? _____

_____.

* * *

calculated t is greater than the table value
for 9 df. Reject the null hypothesis!

---

31. If we reject the null hypothesis (i.e., there is no difference between the two means) we then verify that the second mean was, in fact, greater than the first mean.

What could you then conclude about the tennis class? _____

_____

_____.

* * *

that there was a significant improvement
from test 1 to test 2

32. A teacher gave a basketball free throwing test at the beginning and at the end of a basketball unit of instruction. Here are the scores:

Plate 81

first test	second test	D	D^2
16	15		
14	16		
9	13		
11	9		
13	12		
12	12		
9	10		
10	9		
		$\Sigma D =$	$\Sigma D^2 =$

Find: a. $\Sigma D =$ $\bar{X}_1 =$ $N =$
$\Sigma D^2 =$ $\bar{X}_2 =$
b. $t =$

$$t = \frac{\bar{X}_1 - \bar{X}_2}{\sqrt{\frac{\Sigma D^2 - \frac{(\Sigma D)^2}{N}}{N(N-1)}}}$$

c. $df =$
d. was there a significant improvement in basketball free shooting ability?

* * *

a. $\Sigma D = 2$ $\bar{X}_1 = 11.75$ $N = 8$
$\Sigma D^2 = 28$ $\bar{X}_2 - 12.0$
b. $t = .36$

$$t = \frac{11.75 - 12.0}{\sqrt{\frac{28 - \frac{(2)^2}{8}}{8(8-1)}}}$$

c. $df = N - 1$, or 7
d. no!

EXERCISES FOR SET 11

1. Jack and Sam teach in a high school. Jack feels that his students are better fit than Sam's students. They decide on a test, administer it to their classes, and receive the following scores:

Jack's Class		Sam's Class	
X_1	X_1^2	X_2	X_2^2
11		6	
10		8	
6		8	
8		7	
11		12	
9		13	
13		9	
12		12	
6		8	
7		6	
7		10	
5		11	
		7	

   Find: a. $\Sigma X_1 =$ $\quad n_1 =$
   $\quad\quad\quad \Sigma X_2 =$ $\quad n_2 =$
   $\quad\quad\quad \Sigma X_1^2 =$ $\quad \bar{X}_1 =$
   $\quad\quad\quad \Sigma X_2^2 =$ $\quad \bar{X}_2 =$

   b. $t =$
   c. $df =$
   d. Was one group better than the other? (Use a probability level of .05.)

2. A teacher believes that by placing his physical education class on a leg strength program, he can increase their speed in running the 60 yard dash. He administers a sprint test at the beginning of the semester, involves the students in a rigorous leg strength development program, then retests them on sprinting 8 weeks later.

first test times	second test times	D	D^2
7.6	7.2		
8.9	8.6		
10.1	10.0		
9.7	9.7		
9.1	9.0		
8.5	8.4		
8.2	8.0		
8.4	8.2		
10.0	9.7		
7.9	7.5		

Find: a. $\Sigma D =$ $\bar{X}_1 =$ $N =$
$\Sigma D^2 =$ $\bar{X}_2 =$
b. $t =$

$$t = \frac{\bar{X}_1 - \bar{X}_2}{\sqrt{\dfrac{\Sigma D^2 - \dfrac{(\Sigma D)^2}{N}}{N(N-1)}}}$$

c. $df =$ ($df = N - 1$)
d. Was the training program effective? (Use a probability level of .05.)

ANSWERS FOR SET 11 EXERCISES

1. a. $\Sigma X_1 = 105$ $\quad n_1 = 12$
   $\Sigma X_2 = 117$ $\quad n_2 = 13$
   $\Sigma X_1^2 = 995$ $\quad \bar{X}_1 = 8.75$
   $\Sigma X_2^2 = 1121$ $\quad \bar{X}_2 = 9.0$
   b. $t = .25$
   c. $df = 24$
   d. No, the groups were not really different. We would accept the null hypothesis at the .05 probability level.

2. a. $\Sigma D = -.21$ $\quad \bar{X}_1 = 8.84$ $\quad N = 10$
   $\Sigma D^2 = .61$ $\quad \bar{X}_2 = 8.63$
   b. $t = 2.56$

   $$t = \frac{8.84 - 8.63}{\sqrt{\frac{.61 - \frac{(-.21)^2}{10}}{10(10-1)}}}$$

   c. $df = 9$
   d. yes

SET 12

Graphic Presentation of Data

The statistical procedures presented in this book are useful in many ways. They often become more meaningful, however, if the data are put into some type of graphic form. Graphics highlight the major characteristics of the data for users.

There are numerous kinds of graphs such as circle graphs, frequency polygons, ogive curves, line graphs, pictorial graphs, trilinear graphs, or horizontal and vertical bar graphs. Graphic axes may use arithmetic scales, logarithmic scales or a combination of both.

In this set we will consider the most frequently used kinds of graphs—line graphs and the histogram—using arithmetic scales on each axis.

OBJECTIVES

After completion of this set you will be able to:

1. Identify elements of graphic construction.
2. Graphically display data showing frequency of occurrence.
3. Graphically display data showing improvement of performance.
4. Graphically display data showing comparison between groups.

1. Rectangular coordinate graphs are, by far, most frequently used for graphically displaying data. They are derived by using Quadrant I of a rectangular coordinate system.

216 Using Statistics in Teaching Physical Education

Plate 82

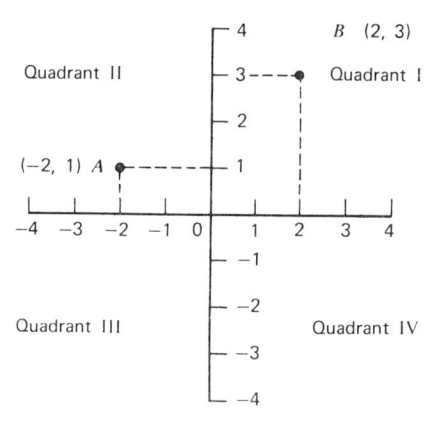

```
                    4      B (2, 3)
    Quadrant II     3---•  Quadrant I
                    2
  (-2, 1) A •------ 1
        -4 -3 -2 -1 0  1  2  3  4
                   -1
                   -2
    Quadrant III          Quadrant IV
                   -3
                   -4
```

In what quadrants are points *A* and *B* found? _____

_____.

* * *

II and I respectively

2. The perpendicular lines forming a rectangular coordinate system are called axes. The horizontal line is called the *X* axis and the vertical line is called the *Y* axis.

More complex graphs may use more than one quadrant, however, most graphs use Quadrant I. In Plate 83, point *B* is located in Quadrant I and has two values; a value of 2 on the *X* axis and _____ on the *Y* axis.

Plate 83

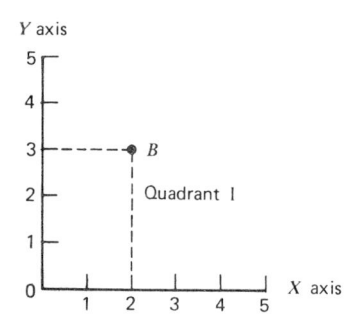

```
        Y axis
        5
        4
        3 -----• B
        2      | Quadrant I
        1      |
        0 ───┴─┴─┴─┴── X axis
           1  2  3  4  5
```

3

3. Each coordinate or axis has a numerical scale of some type. The intersection of the two axes is zero. The numerical scale on each axis can be different; however, the zero point for each scale should be where the two axes intersect. In Plate 84, place a point where the X and Y values are 30 and 9 respectively.

Plate 84

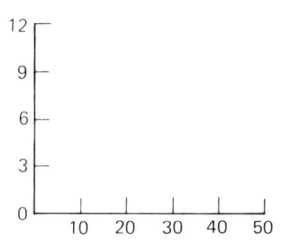

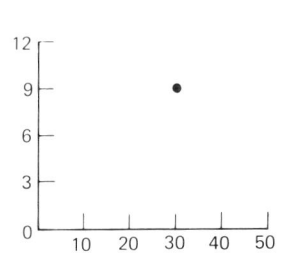

* * *

4. In the previous plates small marks have been placed on the X and Y axes to denote numerical values. These are called ticks. Other methods used on graphs are to use grid lines, and a combination of ticks and grid lines.

218 Using Statistics in Teaching Physical Education

Plate 85

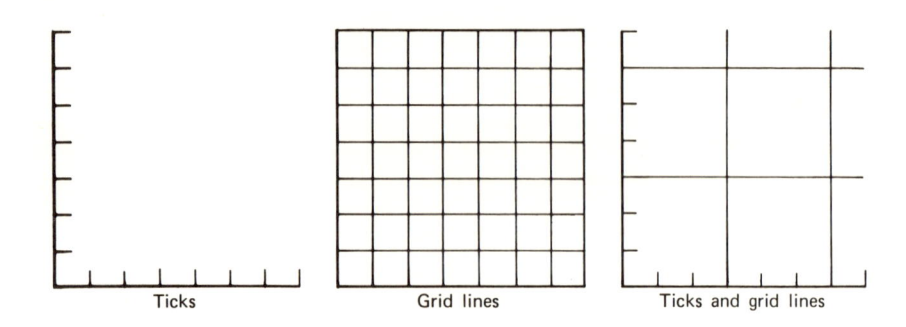

| Ticks | Grid lines | Ticks and grid lines |

Ticks and grid lines are used to _____

_____.

* * *

denote scale values on the axes

5. If scale values are distantly removed from zero, the line should be broken as shown in Plate 86.

To the right of Plate 86 draw a graph where the X axis goes from 0–10 with increments of 2, and the Y axis goes from 100–200 in increments of 20.

Plate 86

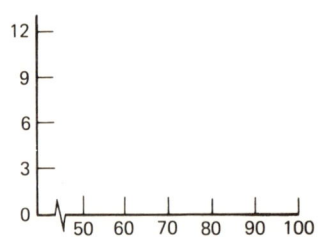

Comparing Group Performance   219

* * *

[Graph with Y-axis labeled "Did you remember to break the Y axis line?" showing values 100, 120, 140, 160, 180, 200 and X-axis values 2, 4, 6, 8, 10, with a break in the Y axis line.]

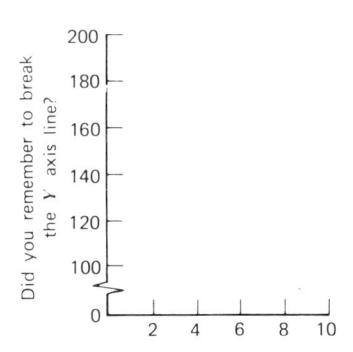

6. Selecting a proportion of height to width of a graph is very important. Data can be distorted by improper proportions. Plate 87 shows the same data plotted with differing ratios of height to width.

Plate 87

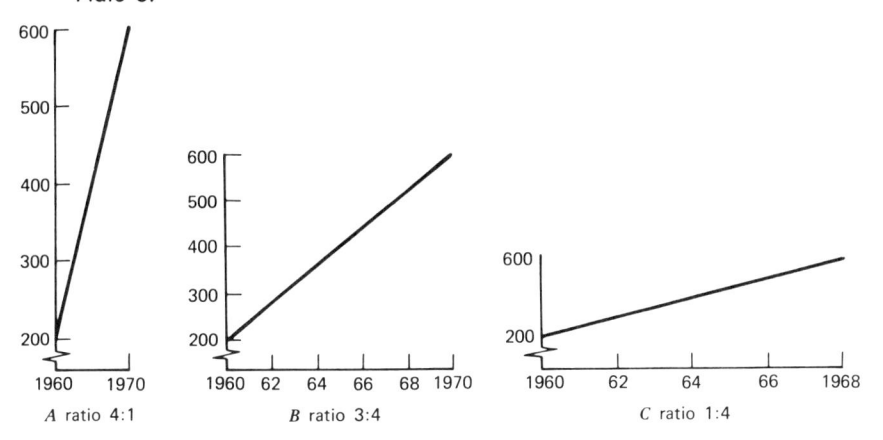

[Three graphs showing the same data with different height-to-width ratios:
A ratio 4:1 (1960–1970, values 200–600)
B ratio 3:4 (1960, 62, 64, 66, 68, 1970, values 200–600)
C ratio 1:4 (1960, 62, 64, 66, 1968, values 200–600)]

Head coaches salaries over a 10 year period (X axis represents time, Y axis represents dollars spent/yr)

If you were a biased coach trying to show how little coaches salaries have increased, which graph ratio would you tend to use to make your point: A, B or C? _____.

* * *

C

7. In most physical education situations, graphs should be constructed so that there is a ratio for the height and width of coordinates of 3:4 or 4:5. (i.e., the height or Y axis would be 3 inches high and the width or X axis of the graph would be 4 inches wide.)

Based on this principle, which graph had the best proportion in Plate 87: A, B or C? _____.

* * *

B

---

8. Graphs should be constructed using appropriate scales and tick marks (and/or grid lines).

The proportion of height to width should be a ratio of approximately what? _____.

* * *

3:4 or 4:5

---

9. Graph lines, regardless of the kind of graph, should be the outstanding feature of the graph. If only one line is shown it is usually a solid line. If more than one line is shown, the second line could be a dotted line, dot-dash line, etc. The main graph line should be the darkest line (or lines) and be of uniform thickness.

Plate 88

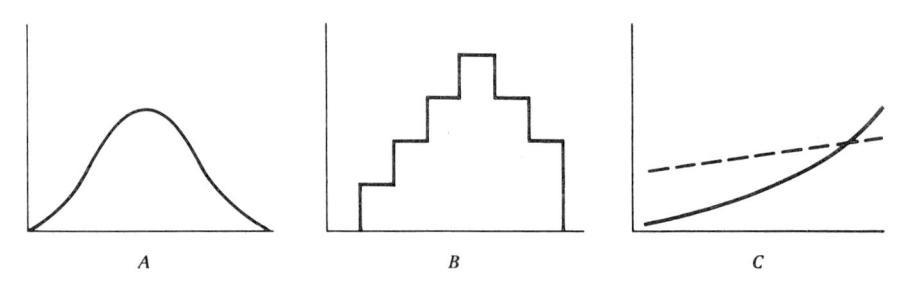

Which graph line would indicate data for more than one group of scores: A, B or C? _____.

* * *

C

10. Construct a frequency polygon graph with an approximate ratio of 3:4 (height to width). Let the Y axis represent weight with a range of 100 to 200 lb. Let the X axis represent grades 8, 9, 10, 11 and 12. The mean weight for boys in the eighth grade was 105, ninth grade—142, tenth grade—169, eleventh grade—185 and twelfth grade—191.

Plot points and connect with a curved line. Use tick marks at each 10 lb on the Y axis and grid lines for each grade level on the X axis. Label each axis.

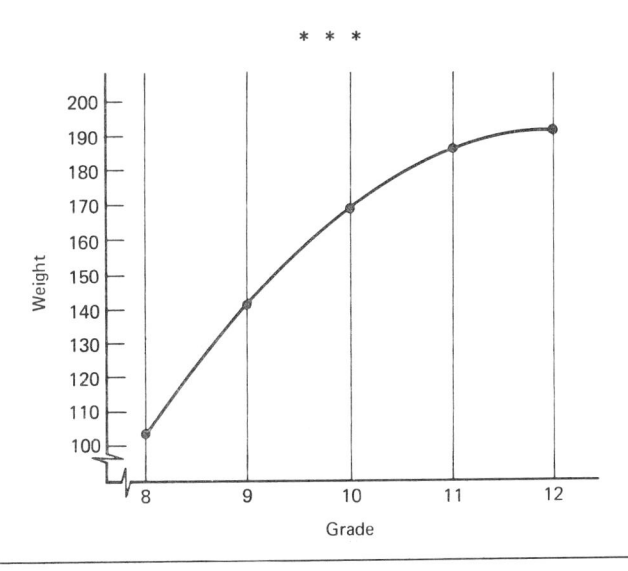

* * *

11. A frequency polygon is a graphic picture of a frequency distribution. The points may be connected and the curve left as is, or the curve may be smoothed or rounded. In Plate 89 a smoothed graph has been constructed using the data in the frequency distribution in Set 7, Frame 16. The midpoint of each interval is used for the X axis. The frequency of scores within each interval is used on the Y axis. A zero is added to each end of the frequency distribution to prevent the curve from appearing to float in air.

Plate 89

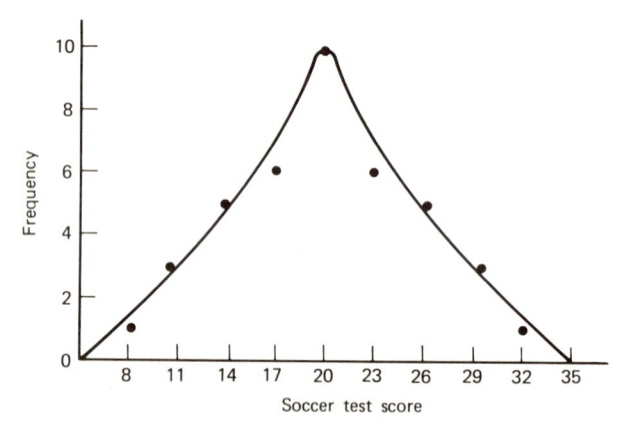

Examine the frequency polygon and answer the following questions:

a. what is the variable for the X axis? _____

_____.

b. what is the variable for the Y axis? _____

_____.

c. does the graph use ticks, grid lines—or both? _____

_____.

* * *

      a. soccer test scores
      b. frequency of occurrence for any score
      c. ticks

12. In your own words describe the use of a frequency polygon.

_____

_____

_____

* * *

Your answer should be something like:
a frequency polygon is used to graphically picture
how scores are distributed in a frequency distribution

13. In a frequency polygon the frequency of occurrence of any given score is noted by which axis? _____.

* * *

the Y axis

14. Another similar graphic method for the presentation of a frequency distribution is the histogram. Rectangles are used here to represent the quantities for each interval. The Y axis is frequency of occurrence and the X axis represents the intervals. Plate 90 shows the same data that were plotted in the frequency polygon of Plate 89. Remember, the actual limits of an interval for a score of 26 is 24.5 and 27.4 when the interval is 3. (Return to Set 7, Frame 13, if this concept is not clear.)

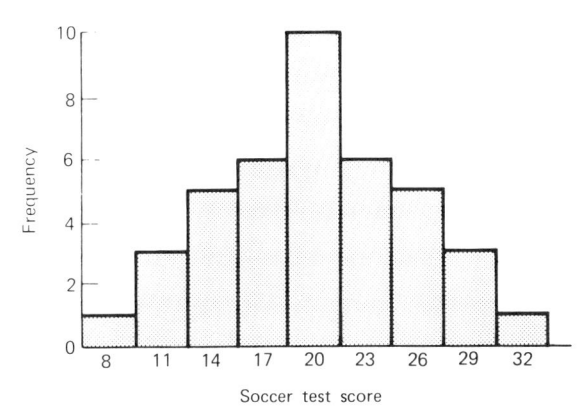

Plate 90

224 Using Statistics in Teaching Physical Education

In the frequency histogram the X axis is established using the _____ rather than the midpoints.

* * *

interval width or size

---

15. Construct a histogram with an approximate ratio of 4:5 (height to width). Let the Y axis represent weight with a range of 100 to 200 lb. Let the X axis represent grades 8, 9, 10, 11 and 12. The mean weights for boys in the eighth grade was 105, ninth grade—142, tenth grade—169, eleventh grade—185, and twelfth grade—191.

Use ticks on the Y axis for each 10 lb interval.

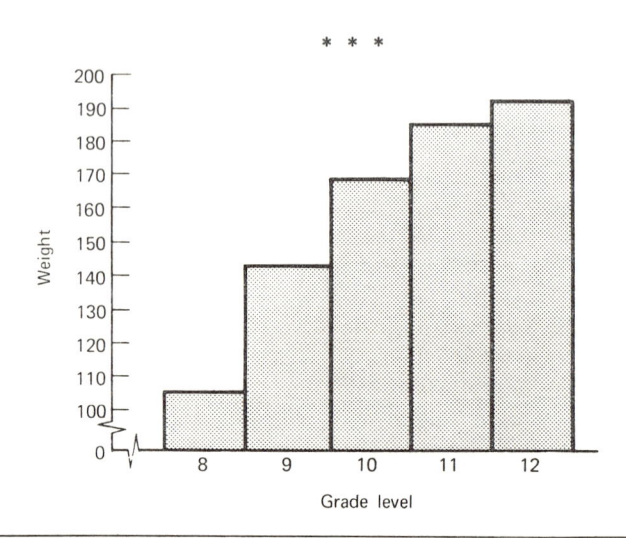

* * *

16. Compare the graphs you completed in Frames 10 and 15. Which kind of frequency graph appears best for the data shown—the frequency polygon or the histogram? _____

* * *

probably the frequency polygon since the weight
ascends only in a curvilinear manner

17. Return to Frame 14, Plate 90, and place the midpoints on the graph for each interval—then connect the midpoints.

* * *

the completed graph should then look like:

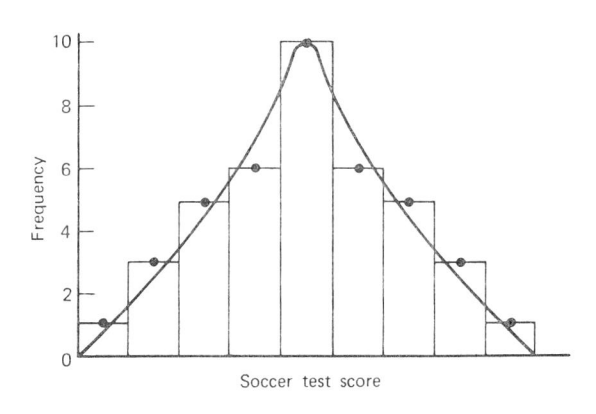

18. Which of the graphs have we discussed and used to graphically portray the way a group of scores are distributed? _____

* * *

frequency polygon, frequency histogram

226 Using Statistics in Teaching Physical Education

19. Line graphs and bar graphs may be used for displaying many kinds of data, in addition to frequencies.

Assume we wished to graphically display class physical fitness improvement throughout the year. We measure pull-ups each month and plot the progress on a graph so that students can visualize their improvement. The data points could be for an individual student or the class mean.

Plate 91

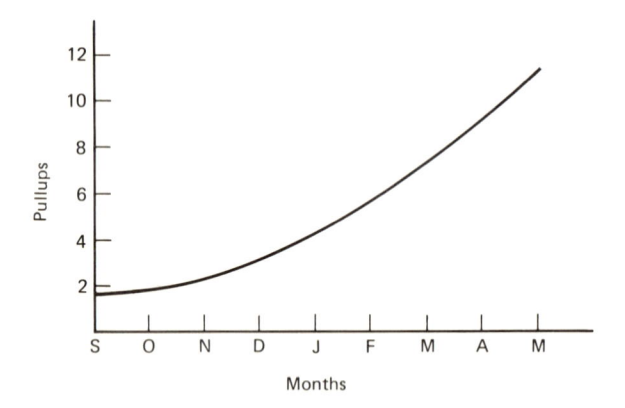

On this line graph, what does the X axis represent? _____

_____.

* * *

time in months or the school year

20. In Plate 91 the graph curve indicates that the students started at a low level, improved rather slowly for a few months, then really improved during the later months of the school year.

If this curve represented the class mean, a dotted line could be plotted showing how any student's progress compared to the progress of the class.

Comparing Group Performance   227

Go back to Plate 91 and add a dotted line showing John's progress. His scores were:

September	4	February	6
October	4	March	7
November	5	April	7
December	5	May	8
January	6		

* * *

the completed graph should look like:

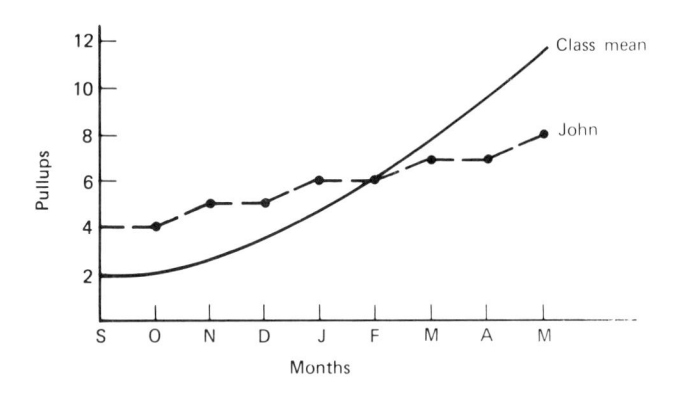

---

21. How would you analyze John's improvement compared to the class mean? _____
   _____.

* * *

> John was stronger at the beginning of the year; however, his improvement was not as great as the class mean

22. You may have noticed that throughout this set most graphs have been labeled in some manner. Each axis should always be labeled. Additional notation should be given for the title of the graph and if more than one line is placed on a graph, the lines should be labeled so that they may be differentiated.

In the graph you constructed in Frame 20, what were the appropriate labels for the X and Y axes? _____

_____.

* * *

X = time in months, Y = the number of pullups

23. What would be an appropriate title for the graph constructed in Frame 20? _____

_____.

* * *

Your answer should be something like:
        gain in ability to do pull-ups for a class and
        one individual between September and May

24. In the graph you constructed in Frame 20, what does the dotted line represent? _____.

* * *

John's progress

25. More complex graphs can be made by using additional lines and/or bars, by using negative quadrants, and by using semi-logarithmetic scales. The principle you have learned can be extended in many ways to form various graphic displays. The principle purpose of graphing data is to enable any data to be more easily interpreted.

The fundamental elements of most graphs are: they use Quadrant I of the rectangular coordinate system; they have X and Y axes or coordinates; each coordinate has a scale of values; each axis has tick marks or grid lines; the coordinate lengths are of reasonable proportions; and the coordinates are labeled.

In your own words describe what the purpose of a graph is. _____
_____
_____.

* * *

Your answer should be something like:
        data are graphed in order to visualize and
        interpret the numerical data more easily

EXERCISES FOR SET 12

1. Complete the following set of matching statements by selecting the response in Column B that best matches the statement in Column A.

	Column A	Column B
___ 1.	Short marks on the axes to denote scale.	A. I
___ 2.	The quadrant of the rectangular coordinate system used most frequently in graph construction.	B. II C. Y axis D. 3:4
___ 3.	The horizontal coordinate.	E. ticks
___ 4.	The proper ratio of height to width of graphs.	F. 4:3 G. X-axis
___ 5.	Most outstanding element of a graph.	H. graph line or curve
___ 6.	Frequency is usually found on which axis?	I. III

2. From the following frequency distribution of push-up scores construct a frequency polygon and a frequency histogram. (Use extra paper.)

Number of Push-Ups	Frequency (Number of Students)
6	1
7	1
8	2
9	4
10	5
11	7
12	8
13	9
14	5
15	2
16	2
17	1
18	1
19	1
20	1

3. Construct a line graph showing how two classes compare on a composite fitness test. The test was given three times during the year—in October, January and April. (Use extra paper.)

Means for Class A		Means for Class B	
October	40	October	50
January	50	January	70
April	60	April	90

ANSWERS FOR SET 12

1.
   1. E
   2. A
   3. G
   4. D
   5. H
   6. C

2.

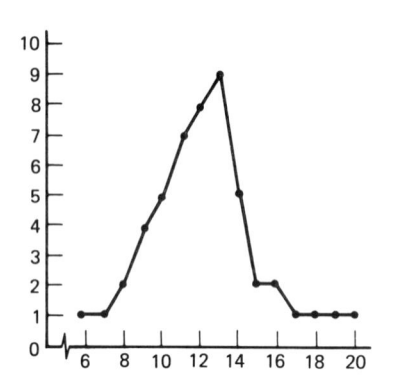

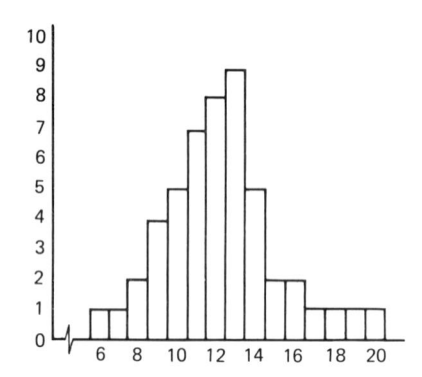

3.

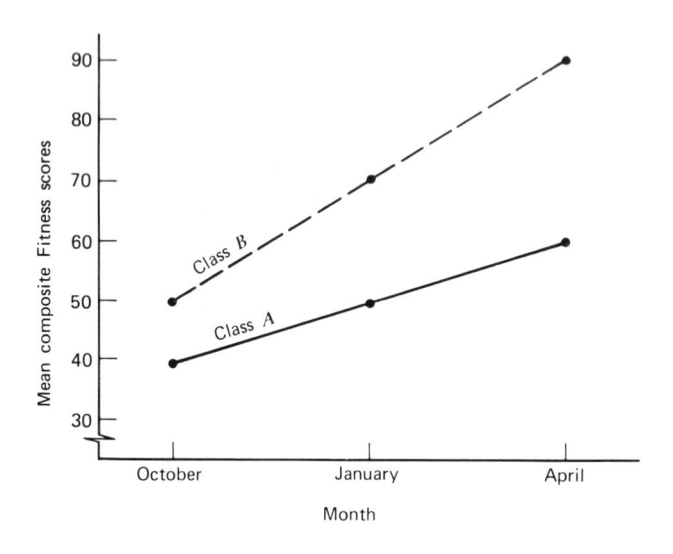

APPENDIX A

Calculation of Square Root

Although square root tables, slide rules and calculators may be available, often we need to calculate the square root of a number.

OBJECTIVES

At the conclusion of this unit a student should be able to calculate the square root of any number.

---

1. The square root of a given number is that quantity when multiplied by itself, equals the original number. The symbol used for square root is $\sqrt{}$.

   Step 1 in calculating the square root of a number is to identify the decimal point of the number—if it is not present. If a decimal point is not shown, it is assumed to be at the right of the number.

   $$\sqrt{625}$$

   Rewrite the above with a decimal point.

$$\sqrt{625.}$$

---

2. Step 2 is to determine how many decimal places you desire in the answer, then add *twice* that many zeros to the right of the decimal point. If you want to carry out our answer to two places, how would you write the previous problem?

$$\sqrt{625.}$$

* * *

$$\sqrt{625.0000}$$

---

3. In Step 3 we raise the decimal point to the quotient or answer. Do this on our problem.

$$\sqrt{625.0000}$$

* * *

$$\sqrt{625.0000}$$

---

4. Step 4 is another mechanical step. We pair off the numbers by two's, both directions from the decimal point. Notice that when moving to the left of the decimal with an odd number of digits, a single digit remains. If you wish, place a zero in front of the single digit in order to have a pair of numbers. (Remember, that does not change the value of the number.)

Add this step to our problem by adding a bar above each *pair* of numbers.

$$\sqrt{625.0000}$$

Calculation of Square Root 237

* * *

$$\sqrt{\overline{06}\ \overline{25}.\overline{00}\ \overline{00}}$$

---

5. Prepare the number 3167 for calculation of its square root by applying the first 4 steps. We will want to carry out the answer to 3 decimal places.

* * *

$$\sqrt{\overline{31}\ \overline{67}.\overline{00}\ \overline{00}\ \overline{00}}$$

---

6. Thus far we have only used whole numbers. The procedures are the same with any number. Prepare the number .07329 for square root calculation. We will carry out the answer to 3 places.

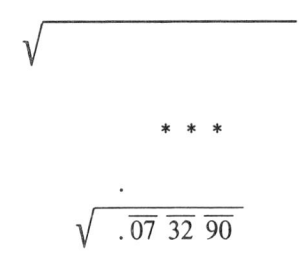

$$\sqrt{}$$

* * *

$$\sqrt{.\overline{07}\ \overline{32}\ \overline{90}}$$

---

7. Set up the number 635.04 for square root calculation. We will carry out the answer to 2 places.

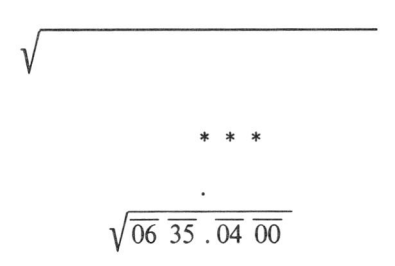

$$\sqrt{}$$

* * *

$$\sqrt{\overline{06}\ \overline{35}.\overline{04}\ \overline{00}}$$

238 Using Statistics in Teaching Physical Education

8. Up to this point we have done no calculation. We have reviewed the four mechanical steps that set the decimal point and the number of digits in the final answer. We can now ignore the placement of the decimal point.

    Now we begin to calculate by working with each pair of numbers starting from the left and working to the right. In Step 5 we estimate the number that, when multiplied by itself, will be just *less* than the first pair of numbers. In our example, what number, when multiplied by itself, will be just less than 6? _____

    $$\sqrt{06\ 35\ .\ 04\ 00}$$

    * * *

    2

9. 3×3=9 is greater than 6, but 2×2=4. Therefore, this is the first number in our answer and is placed above the first bar or pair of numbers.

    $$\sqrt{\overset{2}{06}\ \overset{.}{35}\ .\ 04\ 00}$$

    The product of the least square (4) is placed below the first pair of numbers and subtracted. Carry out this step on the problem below.

    $$\sqrt{\overset{2}{06}\ \overset{.}{35}\ .\ 04\ 00}$$

    * * *

    $$\sqrt{\overset{2}{06}\ \overset{.}{35}\ .\ 04\ 00}$$
    $$\phantom{\sqrt{0}}\underline{\ 4}$$
    $$\phantom{\sqrt{0}}\ 2$$

10. Step 6 involves placing a vertical line downward, doubling the total quotient (the number or numbers above the square root radical) and placing this product to the left of the vertical line, and adding a question mark.

    Example:

$$
\begin{array}{r}
2. \\
\sqrt{06\ 35\ .\ 04\ 00} \\
4
\end{array}
$$

$$4?\ \big|\ 2$$

Placement of the question mark is very important as a reminder that the next divisor will be a two digit number. Step 6 involves drawing a vertical line, doubling the number above the square root radical, and adding a _____ _____ .

* * *

question mark

11. Step 7 involves "bringing down" the next *pair of numbers.*

$$
\begin{array}{r}
2. \\
\sqrt{06\ 35\ .\ 04\ 00} \\
4
\end{array}
$$

$$4?\ \big|\ 235$$

We now estimate the second digit in the answer by guessing how many times 4? will go into 235. Let's guess 5 times. We place the 5

240 Using Statistics in Teaching Physical Education

above the second bar (pair of numbers) and also replace the question mark with the 5.

$$\begin{array}{r} 2\ \ 5\ . \\ \sqrt{06\ \ 35\ .\ 04\ \ 00} \\ 4 \end{array}$$

45 | 235

Then multiply 5×45 to make sure that our estimate does not exceed 235.

$$\begin{array}{r} 2\ \ 5\ . \\ \sqrt{06\ \ 35\ .\ 04\ \ 00} \\ 4 \end{array}$$

45 | 235
     225
     ―――
      10

Would an estimated number of six work? _____ Why or why not? _____.

* * *

No!

$$\begin{array}{r} 2\ \ 6\ . \\ \sqrt{06\ \ 35\ .\ 04\ \ 00} \\ 4 \end{array}$$

46 | 235
     276

276 exceeds 235

―――――――――――――――――――――――――――

12. There is nothing more to learn. Steps 6 and 7 are repeated for each remaining pair of numbers under the square root radical.

Calculation of Square Root

To summarize, Steps 6 and 7:

draw the vertical line
double the total number above the radical
add the question mark
estimate the next number in the answer

Estimate the next number in the sample problem.

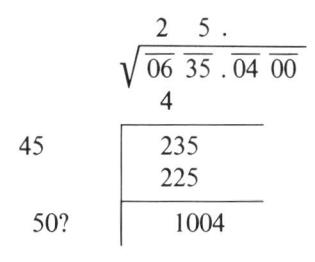

$$\begin{array}{r} 2\ \ 5\ . \\ \sqrt{06\ 35\ .\ 04\ 00} \\ 4 \end{array}$$

45	235
	225
50?	1004

* * *

2

---

13. The final answer then, since there is no remainder, is 25.20.

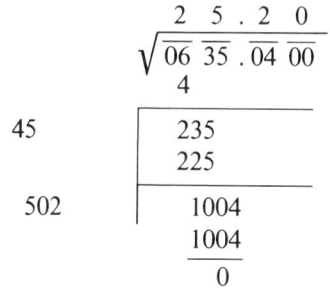

$$\begin{array}{r} 2\ \ 5\ .\ 2\ \ 0 \\ \sqrt{06\ 35\ .\ 04\ 00} \\ 4 \end{array}$$

45	235
	225
502	1004
	1004
	0

Check: 25.2×25.2 = _____ .

* * *

635.04

(always check your number by squaring the answer
to see if the result is your original number)

242 Using Statistics in Teaching Physical Education

14. The procedure is exactly the same for calculating the square root of any number. There are four mechanical steps (1 to 4), one preliminary step to get the calculation started (5) and two final steps (6 and 7) which are repeated until the desired number of decimal points are obtained in the answer. You could make step numbers into a series of three numbers, 4–1–2, to aid memory of the procedure. Perform the first four steps on the number .10304. Set up the problem to be carried out to three decimal places.

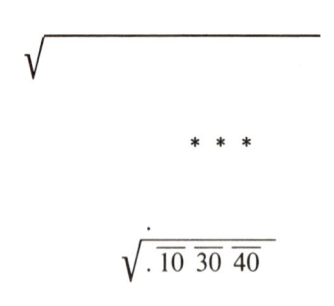

$$\sqrt{}$$

* * *

$$\sqrt{.\overset{.}{10}\ \overline{30}\ \overline{40}}$$

15. Perform the next step (5), which begins the calculation.

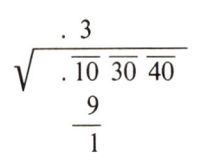

$$\sqrt{.\overset{.}{10}\ \overline{30}\ \overline{40}}$$

* * *

$$\sqrt{\begin{array}{r}.\ \ 3\\ \overline{.\ \overset{.}{10}\ \overline{30}\ \overline{40}}\\ \underline{9}\\ 1\end{array}}$$

16. Finish the problem applying Steps 6 and 7. Carry out to the nearest three places.

Calculation of Square Root

$$\begin{array}{r}.3\\\sqrt{.10\ 30\ 40}\\9\\\hline 1\end{array}$$

* * *

$$\begin{array}{r}.3\ 2\ 1\\\sqrt{.10\ 30\ 40}\\9\\\hline\end{array}$$

62	130
	124
641	640
	641

17. Now calculate the square root of the number 387592. Carry out the answer two decimal places. (Remember the series of steps, 4–1–2.)

$$\sqrt{}$$

```
            6  2  2 . 5  6
         ┌─────────────────
        √ 38 75 92 . 00 00
            36
        ────────
 122      │ 275
          │ 244
        ────────
 1242     │ 3192
          │ 2484
        ────────
 12445    │ 70800
          │ 62225
        ────────
 124506   │ 857500
          │ 747036
```

EXERCISES FOR SQUARE ROOT CALCULATION   APPENDIX A

Find the square root of the following numbers. Carry out to three decimal places in the answers.

1. $\sqrt{1225}$ 4. $\sqrt{.7286}$

2. $\sqrt{982.765}$ 5. $\sqrt{.00073}$

3. $\sqrt{5}$

ANSWERS FOR SQUARE ROOT CALCULATION   APPENDIX A

1. 35.000
2. 31.349
3. 2.236
4. .853
5. .027

APPENDIX B
Elementary Algebraic Procedures

This unit briefly reviews elementary concepts necessary for the solution of simple problems in algebra. If you can meet the objectives of this unit and those in Appendix A, you shoiuld be able to solve any problem in this program.

OBJECTIVES

At the completion of this unit the student will be able to:

1. Recall the names for parts of arithmetic problems.
2. Be able to add, subtract, multiply and divide positive and negative numbers.
3. Know the order of operation for solving simple equations.

---

1. When adding a group of numbers, each individual number is called an addend. This is easy to remember because the first syllable refers to the operation in progress.

    In the following problem, what are the individual numbers called?

    _____.

    $$36 + 48 + 12 =$$

250 Using Statistics in Teaching Physical Education

* * *

addends

---

2. The addends are added to give the sum of the group of numbers. In the problem 6+14+3=23, the number 23 is called the _____.

* * *

sum

---

3. In the problem below, what are the numbers above the line called? _____.

What is the number below the line called? _____.

$$\begin{array}{r} 364 \\ 248 \\ 632 \\ \hline 1244 \end{array}$$

* * *

addends, sum

---

4. In subtraction, the original number you have is called the minuend (you start with a dance—the minuet!) The number subtracted from that original number is called the subtrahend. The answer is called the difference.

If we subtract 22 from 44, the number 22 is called the _____.

* * *

subtrahend

---

5. The word subtrahend can be remembered because the first two syllables describe the operation in progress. The subtrahend is subtracted from the _____.

Elementary Algebraic Procedures 251

* * *

minuend

---

6. When the subtrahend is subtracted from the minuend, the result is called the _____.

* * *

difference

---

7. Label the parts of the following subtraction problem.

$$\begin{array}{r}268 \\ \underline{124} \\ 144\end{array}$$ _____

* * *

$$\begin{array}{rl}268 & \text{minuend} \\ \underline{124} & \text{subtrahend} \\ 144 & \text{difference}\end{array}$$

---

8. In multiplication, the number being multiplied is called the multiplicand. The number you multiply by is called the multiplier. The answer is called the product.

   In the following problem, which number is the multiplier? _____.

$$34 \times 6 = 204$$

* * *

6

---

9. In multiplication, the product is found by multiplying the multiplier by the _____.

multiplicand

---

10. The answer in a multiplication problem is called the _____.

* * *

product

---

11. Label the parts of the following multiplication problem:

$365 \times 32 = 11680$ or
$$\begin{array}{r} 365 \\ \times 32 \\ \hline 11680 \end{array}$$

     365   _____
     × 32   _____
    11680   _____

* * *

365   multiplicand
32   multiplier
11680 product

---

12. In division you have a number that you want to divide by another number. The number you want to divide is called the dividend. Remember this term by thinking of a stock dividend check and how it can be split up to be spent on various items. The divisor is the number by which you divide and the answer is called the quotient.

In the following problems, what numbers are the dividends?

$$\frac{64}{2} = 32 \qquad 32 \div 16 = 2 \qquad 4\overline{)16}^{4}$$

* * *

64, 32, 16

Elementary Algebraic Procedures   253

13. In the problem $\frac{32}{16} = 2$, the 16 is the _____ and the 2 is the _____.

* * *

divisor, quotient

14. Label the parts of the following division problem:

$$528 \div 33 = 16 \quad \text{or} \quad \frac{528}{33} = 16 \text{ _____}$$

* * *

$$\frac{528}{33} = 16 \quad \begin{array}{l} \text{dividend} \\ \text{quotient} \\ \text{divisor} \end{array}$$

15. In algebra we are continually dealing with common fractions. Fractions are numbers that show part of a whole thing or group of things. A fraction is made up of top numbers and bottom numbers called terms, with a fraction line between them.

A fraction is really, then, a division problem with a dividend and a divisor. However, to complicate matters when dealing with fractions we used different names: the dividend is called the numerator and the divisor is called the denominator.

In the following equation, which term is the numerator—the term above the line or the term below the line? _____.

$$\frac{6D^2}{N(N^2-1)}$$

* * *

above the line
(notice that the numerator can be more than one number!)

16. An easy way to remember these relationships is to memorize the following:

$$\frac{\text{dividend} = \text{numerator}}{\text{divisor} = \text{denominator}}$$

In the following equation, what term is the denominator? _____.

$$\bar{X} = \frac{\Sigma X}{N}$$

* * *

N

---

17. In the equation $\bar{X} = \frac{\Sigma X}{N}$, the ΣX is the _____.

* * *

numerator

---

18. In the equation $\bar{X} = \frac{\Sigma X}{N}$, which term represents the quotient? _____.

* * *

$\bar{X}$

---

19. Often we must work with numbers that are less than zero. So, we must use rules for working with signed numbers, that is, positive and negative numbers (+5, −5).

Positive numbers may have a plus sign in front of them. If there is no sign in front of a number, it is considered to be a positive number. If a number is a negative number, it *must* have a minus sign in front of it.

How many positive figures are shown below?_____.

+5   r   13   −6   −236

* * *

3 (+5 r 13)

---

20. In adding numbers where the signs are the same, merely add the numbers and attach the common sign to the sum.

    Apply this rule to the following:

    a. $\begin{array}{r} +\ 7 \\ +11 \\ \hline \end{array}$ b. $\begin{array}{r} -4 \\ -7 \\ \hline \end{array}$ c. $(-5)+(-4)=$

    * * *

    a. 18   b. -11 c. -9

---

21. When adding numbers where the signs are not the same, find the difference between the sum of the plus numbers and the sum of the minus numbers, and attach the sign of the larger.

    Apply this rule to the following:

    a. $\begin{array}{r} +9 \\ -5 \\ \hline \end{array}$ b. $\begin{array}{r} +3 \\ -5 \\ -3 \\ +4 \\ \hline \end{array}$ c. $(+7)+(+1)+(-3)+(5)=$

    * * *

    a. $+4$ b. -1 c. 10

---

22. When subtracting signed numbers, change the sign of the subtrahend, then proceed as in addition.

    Change the sign in the following problem and apply this rule to find the difference.

    $$\text{subtract } \begin{array}{r} +11 \\ +\ 6 \\ \hline \end{array}$$

* * *

$$+11$$
$$-\ 6$$
$$+\ 5$$

---

23. The sign of the subtrahend (+6) was changed to a (−6), then you proceeded to add the signed numbers to get the difference.

    Solve the following subtraction problems:

    a. $\begin{array}{r}+14\\+\ 5\\\hline\end{array}$ b. $\begin{array}{r}+16\\-\ 8\\\hline\end{array}$ c. $34-(-16)=$

    * * *

    a. +9   b. +24   c. +50

---

24. There is a common rule for multiplication and division regarding signed numbers. If the signs are the same, the answer is positive. If the signs are different, the quotient or product is negative. Answer the following questions related to signs in multiplication.

    a. A plus times a plus is a _____.
    b. A minus times a minus is a _____.
    c. A plus times a minus is a _____.

    * * *

    a. plus   b. plus   c. minus

---

25. These same rules apply to division. Apply the rule to the following division situations.

    a. A plus divided by a minus is a _____.
    b. A minus divided by a minus is a _____.
    c. A plus divided by a plus is a _____.

    * * *

    a. minus   b. plus   c. plus

---

26. In order to check your progress, solve the following:

a. (+3) times (−4)
b. (−13) times 5
c. (−49) ÷ (−7)
d. (−16) times (−4)

e. $\dfrac{-36}{+6}$

f. $\dfrac{-144}{-12}$

* * *

a. −12   d. +64
b. −65   e. −6
c. 7   f. 12

27. Often numbers being multiplied are put in parentheses or brackets for clarity, for example (−5) and [−5]. In multiplication, there are two common ways to show that the number within the brackets or parentheses are multiplied.

$$(5)\cdot(-6) \quad \text{and} \quad (5)(-6)$$

In the first example, a dot is placed between the sets of parentheses and in the second case there is nothing between the parentheses. Solve the following:

a. (15)(−3)   b. (−7)(−3)   c. (24)(−2)

* * *

a. −45   b. 21   c. −48

28. A brief review should be made regarding the use of zero. Adding or subtracting zero to any number does not change the number. However, whenever you multiply a number by zero the product becomes zero. Zero divided by any number equals zero.

Solve the following:

a. $376 + 0 =$ b. $210 - 0 =$ c. $56\ (0) =$ d. $\dfrac{0}{32} =$

* * *

a. 376 b. 210 c. 0 d. 0

---

29. When solving formulas, certain calculations must be made before others. The order in which the operations are to be carried out are indicated by parentheses and brackets. Terms within a set of parentheses or brackets must be calculated before the remaining operations are made. Solve the innermost parentheses first.

    In the following example, what would be the order of operation?

    $$[6\,(13-7)]\,[14-3] =$$

    a. Find $(13-7)$ which is 6.
    b.
    c.

    * * *

    b. Find $6\,(13-7)$ which is 6×6 or 36.
    c. Multiply $36\,(11)$.

---

30. There are also definite rules for the removal of parentheses and brackets pertaining to the signs of the numbers involved. When an expression within parentheses is preceded by a plus sign, the parentheses may be removed without making any change in the expression.

    Example:

    $$36 + (32 - 10)$$

    $$36 + 32 - 10$$

    Remove the parentheses from the following:

    $$13 + (100 - 30) + 36 + (7 - 4)$$

Elementary Algebraic Procedures 259

* * *

$$13+100-30+36+7-4$$

---

31. When an expression within parentheses is preceded by a minus sign, the parentheses may be removed if the sign of *every* term within the parentheses is changed.

    Example: $36-(5+8-1)$ becomes $36-5-8+1$

    Remove the parentheses from the following:

    $$64-(-32+13-4)$$

    * * *

    $$64+32-13+4$$

---

32. Now, keeping the rules concerning removal of parentheses and order of operations, collect the terms for the following problem:

    $$[4-(-16+7)]-[(8-1)+(3-2)]=?$$

    * * *

    5

---

33. Also, there is a priority in order of procedure depending on the kind of arithmetic operation. All multiplication and division should be conducted before numbers are added or subtracted.

    For example, in the expression $\left(\frac{8}{2}\right)7+3$

    The quotient 4 is multiplied by 7 then the product (28) is added to 3.

    Solve: a. $\left(\frac{36}{6}\right)8+64=$ b. $\left(\frac{16}{-32}\right)6+30=$

    * * *

    a. $=112$ b. $=27$

34. What would be the order of operation for the following:

$$p = \frac{\left(\frac{17-11}{3}\right)5+9}{40}$$

a.

b.

c.

d.

* * *

a. Solve $\frac{17-11}{3}$, which is 2.
b. Multiply 2·5, which is 10.
c. Add 9 to the 10, which is 19.
d. Divide 19 by 40.

EXERCISES FOR APPENDIX B

1. Label the parts of the following problems:

Addition	Subtraction
3 + 19 = 22	36 − 15 = 21
a. b.	c. d. e.
Multiplication	Division
−35 (7) = −245	81 ÷ 9 = 9
f. g. h.	i. j. k.

2. Which is above the line on a fraction—the numerator or denominator?

3. Make the following calculations with the correct signs:
   a. $13+(-7)+3+(-12)=$

   b. $-33-(-15)=$

   c. $(25)(-3)=$

   d. $\dfrac{-121}{-11}=$

4. Solve the following:
   a.
   $$9\left(\dfrac{-36}{6}+13\right)=$$

   b.
   $$\dfrac{16-14}{\left[32-\left(\dfrac{(8)^2}{-4}\right)\right]\left[\dfrac{1}{10}\right]}=$$

   c.
   $$\dfrac{15.8-20}{\left[3-\left(\dfrac{16}{-2}+6\right)\right][-6(7)]}=$$

ANSWERS FOR EXERCISES IN APPENDIX B

1. a. addend
   b. sum
   c. minuend
   d. subtrahend
   e. difference
   f. multiplicand
   g. multiplier
   h. product
   i. dividend
   j. divisor
   k. quotient

2. Numerator

3. a. −3
   b. −18
   c. −75
   d. 11

4. a. 63
   b. .42
   c. .02

APPENDIX C
Formulas

1. $\bar{X} = \dfrac{\Sigma X}{N}$ Set 3   f 20

2. $R =$ highest value $-$ lowest value $+$ sensitivity   Set 4   f 4

3. $AD = \dfrac{\Sigma(\bar{X} - X)^2}{N}$ Set 4   f 16

4. $\sigma = \sqrt{\dfrac{\Sigma(\bar{X} - X)^2}{N}}$ Set 4   f 20

5. $\sigma = \sqrt{\dfrac{\Sigma X^2}{N} - \bar{X}^2}$ Set 4   f 24

6. $\sigma = 1 - \dfrac{6\Sigma D^2}{N(N^2 - 1)}$ Set 5   f 10

7. $r = \dfrac{N\Sigma XY - (\Sigma X)(\Sigma Y)}{\sqrt{[N\Sigma X^2 - (\Sigma X)^2][N\Sigma Y^2 - (\Sigma Y)^2]}}$ Set 5   f 22

8. $z = \dfrac{X - \bar{X}}{\sigma}$ Set 6   f 28

9. $c_{\text{sigma}} = \dfrac{3.0\sigma}{50}$ Set 6   f 44

10. $c_{\text{Hull}} = \dfrac{3.5\sigma}{50}$ Set 3   f 44

11. $c_T = \dfrac{5.0\sigma}{50}$ Set 6   f 44

12. $\overline{X} = \Sigma \overline{X} + \left(\dfrac{\Sigma fd}{N} \cdot i\right)$ Set 7   f 27

13. $\sigma = i\sqrt{\dfrac{\Sigma fd^2}{N} - \left(\dfrac{\Sigma fd}{N}\right)^2}$ Set 7   f 30

14. $r = \dfrac{\dfrac{\Sigma\Sigma fm}{N} - (c_x \cdot c_y)}{\sigma_x \cdot \sigma_y}$ Set 8   f 22

15. $c_x = \dfrac{\Sigma d_x}{N}$ Set 8   f 32

16. $c_y = \dfrac{\Sigma d_y}{N}$ Set 8   f 32

17. $\sigma_x = \sqrt{\dfrac{\Sigma fd_x^2}{N} - c_x^2}$ Set 8   f 33

18. $\sigma_y = \sqrt{\dfrac{\Sigma fd_y^2}{N} - c_y^2}$ Set 8   f 33

19. $X_{.80} = ll + \left(\dfrac{.8N - f_b}{f_w}\right) i$ Set 9   f 14

20. $P_x = \dfrac{\left(\dfrac{X - ll}{i}\right) f_w + f_b}{N}$ Set 9   f 32

21. $t = \dfrac{\overline{X}_1 - \overline{X}_2}{\sqrt{\left[\dfrac{\Sigma X_1^2 - \dfrac{(\Sigma X_1)^2}{n_1} + \Sigma X_2^2 - \dfrac{(\Sigma X_2)^2}{n_2}}{(n_1 + n_2) - 2}\right]\left[\dfrac{1}{n_1} + \dfrac{1}{n_2}\right]}}$

     Set 11   f 4

22. $$t = \frac{\bar{X}_1 - \bar{X}_2}{\sqrt{\dfrac{\Sigma D^2 - \dfrac{(\Sigma D)^2}{N}}{N(N-1)}}}$$ Set 11 f 24

Index